TECHNOLOGY AND CIVIC ENGAGEMENT IN THE COLLEGE CLASSROOM

TECHNOLOGY AND CIVIC ENGAGEMENT IN THE COLLEGE CLASSROOM

Engaging the Unengaged

Edited by

Suzanne M. Chod, William J. Muck,
and Stephen M. Caliendo

TECHNOLOGY AND CIVIC ENGAGEMENT IN THE COLLEGE CLASSROOM
Copyright © Suzanne M. Chod, William J. Muck, and Stephen M. Caliendo, 2015.

All rights reserved.

First published in 2015 by
PALGRAVE MACMILLAN®
in the United States—a division of St. Martin's Press LLC,
175 Fifth Avenue, New York, NY 10010.

Where this book is distributed in the UK, Europe and the rest of the world,
this is by Palgrave Macmillan, a division of Macmillan Publishers Limited,
registered in England, company number 785998, of Houndmills,
Basingstoke, Hampshire RG21 6XS.

Palgrave Macmillan is the global academic imprint of the above companies
and has companies and representatives throughout the world.

Palgrave® and Macmillan® are registered trademarks in the United States,
the United Kingdom, Europe and other countries.

ISBN: 978–1–137–53855–0

Library of Congress Cataloging-in-Publication Data

Technology and civic engagement in the college classroom : engaging the
unengaged / edited by Suzanne M. Chod, William J. Muck,
Stephen M. Caliendo.
        pages cm
    Summary: "Technology and Civic Engagment in the College Clasroom is a
theoretical and empirical examination of ways to foster civic engagement in
Millennials. Each chapter contributes to understanding how both traditional
and more innovative pedagogical tools can increase students' political interest
and efficacy"—Provided by publisher.
    Includes bibliographical references.
    ISBN 978–1–137–53855–0 (hardback)
    1. Civics—Study and teaching (Higher)—United States. 2. Social
media—Political aspects—United States. 3. Service learning—United States.
4. Blended learning—United States. I. Chod, Suzanne M., editor of compilation.
II. Muck, William J., editor of compilation. III. Caliendo, Stephen M., 1971–
editor of compilation.

LC1091.T45 2015
320.4071173—dc23   2015013958

A catalogue record of the book is available from the British Library.

Design by Newgen Knowledge Works (P) Ltd., Chennai, India.

First edition: October 2015

10 9 8 7 6 5 4 3 2 1

To those who never forget why we do what we do and the difference we can make
—Suzanne M. Chod

To my loving family, who always reminds me of what is truly important in life
—William J. Muck

For my many mentors, whose dedication to fostering engagement has, in turn, benefited my students and their communities
—Stephen M. Caliendo

Contents

List of Illustrations   ix

Introduction   1
Suzanne M. Chod and William J. Muck

1   Taking College-Level Political Science Courses
    and Civic Activity   13
    Kenneth W. Moffett and Laurie L. Rice

2   Civic and Political Engagement Outcomes in
    Online and Face-to-Face Courses   49
    Tanya Buhler Corbin and Allison K. Wisecup

3   Rethinking the Way We Communicate about
    Politics with Millennials   89
    Hillary C. Shulman

4   Social Networking as a Pedagogical Tool: Effect
    of Twitter Use on Interest and Efficacy in
    Introductory-Level American Government Courses   123
    Stephen M. Caliendo, Suzanne M. Chod,
    William J. Muck, and Deron Schreck

5   Effectively Using Facebook to Foster Civic
    Engagement   147
    Leah A. Murray

Conclusion   173
Suzanne M. Chod and William J. Muck

List of Contributors   179

Index   183

Illustrations

Figures

1.1 Contacting government officials and taking a political science course   32

1.2 Contacting newspapers and taking a political science course   33

1.3 Participating in protests and taking a political science course   33

Tables

1.1 Civic activities and political science course enrollment   28

1.2 Summary statistics for political science course variables   37

1.3 Frequency of government contact, media contact, and participation in Marches or other similar political activities   38

1.4 Correlation matrix among items in the peer civic experiences index   40

2.1 Descriptive statistics for variables in analysis by type of course   67

2.2 Ordinary Least Squares (OLS) regression models predicting change in internal political efficacy   69

2.3 Ordinary Least Squares (OLS) regression models predicting change in future civic engagement   70

2.4 Ordinary Least Squares (OLS) regression models predicting change in future political engagement   72

2.5 Internal political efficacy indicators   79

2.6 Measures of students' civic and political engagement 80
2.7 Measures of students' political contexts 81
2.8 Sociodemographic measures 82
4.1 Portrait of participants (pretest) 132
4.2 Changes in interest and efficacy, aggregate 135
4.3 Changes in interest and efficacy, individual-level 137
5.1 Posts on assignments 153
5.2 Current events outcome in percentages 154
5.3 Current events rating on rubric 154
5.4 Types of posts 155
5.5 Learning outcome by assignment type 156
5.6 Civic engagement rating by overall
    assignment type 157
5.7 Civic engagement rating by post for discussion 158
5.8 Civic engagement rating by post for Facebook 158

Introduction

Suzanne M. Chod and William J. Muck

The results of the American Political Science Association Task Force's examination of civic education in the United States revealed inadequacies and called upon those who teach politics to act (APSA Task Force on Civic Engagement in the 21st Century 1998). The empirical studies of the declining levels of civic engagement, political knowledge, and efficacy of young people (Delli Carpini 2000; Galston 2004, 2007; Levine and Lopez 2002; Miller and Shanks 1996; Putnam 2000; Wattenberg 2002) along with the APSA Task Force recommendations, inform us that more must be done on the part of political science educators to engage the unengaged. In particular, because political socialization can solidify in college (Newcomb et al. 1967; Niemi and Jennings 1991), instructors can use the classroom as a platform to incite civic engagement and enthusiasm. With this as the case, the next question must be: how can this be done? What strategies and pedagogical tools can instructors use to foster civic engagement?

With a renewed commitment to civic education, scholars began conducting research on varying pedagogical tools that may increase civic engagement, efficacy, and political knowledge. The existing empirical literature has two dominant lines. The first line studies the effect of college and university service learning on civic engagement (Astin and Sax 1998; Birge,

Beaird, and Torres 2003; Hunter and Brisbin 2000; Levine 2007; McCartney 2006; Perry and Katula 2001; Prentice 2007; Spiezio, Baker, and Boland 2005; Yates and Youniss 1998). The second examines how the traditional classroom environment can stimulate civic engagement (Campbell 2008; Hibbing and Theiss-Morse 1996; Niemi and Junn 1998). The first line speaks only as to what institutions can do to increase civic engagement, but provides no insight as to what instructors can do in their classrooms. The second line, while helpful to instructors, fails to account for a changing generation of students, students who see the virtual world as their community and technology as a means to learn and engage. Might the infusion of technology in the classroom help encourage students to be active citizens?

As of late, political science instructors have begun using technology alongside traditional classroom activities and assessments to "speak to" an increasingly technological generation. Using Twitter to engage students with each other and the larger political world, creating assignments on Facebook, using online course technology and assignments, and being strategic in the ways in which political messages are conveyed to students all utilize different pedagogical tools and theories with one goal in mind: helping increase civic engagement, efficacy, and knowledge among college students. These same technologies are also redefining how faculty see and approach their professional development (Carpenter and Drezner 2010).

While a significant amount of literature suggests that the Internet generally (Bennett and Fielding 1999; Bimber 2001; Browning 1996; Dertouzos 1997; Grossman 1995; Johnson and Kaye 1998; Katz and Rice 2002; Morris 2000; Negroponte 1995; Norris 1999, 2001) and social networking sites such as Facebook (Ellison, Steinfield, and Lampe 2007; Lampe, Ellison, and Steinfeld 2006; Pasek, More, and Romer 2009; Steinfield, Ellison, and Lampe 2008; Valenzuela, Park, and Kee 2009; Gil de Zúñiga, Jung, and Valenzuela 2012) can affect areas of civic engagement, there are very few studies that find empirical evidence that using specific types of Web 2.0 technologies in the classroom can achieve this goal (Bukovchik and Chadha 2013; Eikenberry 2012; Greenhow and Gleason 2012; Junco, Heiberger, and Loken 2011). It is this lack of scholarship that inspired this book.

Technology and Civic Engagement in the College Classroom: Engaging the Unengaged is a theoretically driven and empirical contribution to an emerging field of study in political science. The work in this edited volume provides pedagogical justifications for the use of certain technologies and strategies to increase civic engagement that are rooted in political science theory. There are different strategies, both technological and traditional, that can foster civic engagement. This book focuses on both in-class and online ways political science instructors have developed and tested strategies to engage an increasingly unengaged college student population. Increasing civic engagement is not something that can solely be done with technology, but rather it is about a more hybrid pedagogical approach that includes an open classroom environment and class discussion, as well as new technological inclusions that tap into what helps motivate Millennials to connect.

The authors in this collection turn their attention toward additional, direct assessment of the ways that technology in the postsecondary classroom might serve as a catalyst for civic engagement. In chapter 1, Kenneth W. Moffett and Laurie L. Rice begin with the fundamental question of whether taking a college- or university-level course in political science can increase civic activity. Focusing on four specific and differing forms of civic engagement, the authors survey undergraduate students and bolster the widely held belief that taking a course in political science is positively connected with increased levels of civic engagement. Moffett and Rice's findings build upon the extensive research on civic engagement in the classroom. Additionally, their use of more "solitary" forms of civic engagement, such as contacting government officials and newspapers, suggests that civic engagement can be expressed through both individual and collective mechanisms.

While Moffett and Rice's central research question falls squarely within the more traditional literature of examining how the college classroom can foster civic engagement, they are also interested in the connection between online and offline sources of civic engagement. Specifically, they argue that students who engage in meaningful online political expression will be more likely to participate in offline forms of civic engagement. To test this relationship, the authors asked participants questions to gauge the degree to which they participated in online activities, and then connect those online activities to established measures of civic engagement. Their positive finding that online political activity can translate into heightened levels of offline civic engagement is an important contribution to the literature. It suggests that virtual political activity can directly promote more conventional forms of offline civic engagement. The authors force us to think more deeply about the ways in which faculty can infuse online political activities into their pedagogy for the traditional classroom as a way of fostering civic engagement.

Tanya B. Corbin and Allison K. Wisecup push the conversation fully online in chapter 2 with a study comparing efforts at civic engagement in face-to-face and online classes. They argue that we currently know very little about whether online political science courses will be able to nurture civic engagement in the same ways as conventional face-to-face classes. The dramatic and sustained proliferation of online learning presents a monumental challenge to scholars grappling with questions of how to foster civic engagement. The online education community has paid significant attention to assessing learning goals and outcomes, but has not devoted the same attention to questions of civic engagement. While it may be the case that student learning is as strong, if not more effective, in an online environment, the authors argue that more empirical scholarship is needed to examine whether that same trend is visible for fostering civic engagement.

Corbin and Wisecup take an important first step toward addressing that gap. Using a quasi-experimental design the authors administered pre- and posttest surveys to face-to-face and online sections of introductory American government courses. While the data provide mixed results, their overall conclusion is that online political science courses can be just as effective, if not more effective, at developing levels of civic engagement. The findings suggest that both face-to-face and online classes can be powerful tools for fostering civic engagement, which are consistent with other findings in this collection. The message is clear: when properly designed, technology offers exciting opportunities for fostering civic engagement in the classroom. Yet we must be cautious to not simply assume that "more technology" will automatically bring about the desired results. Scholars must explore the strategic ways in which technology can be best utilized. The ways that we use technology matter.

Hillary C. Shulman offers an interdisciplinary look at how the field of communication grapples with questions of civic engagement in chapter 3. The author endeavors to flip the frame and focus more narrowly on the causal factors behind the disengagement of the politically deficient Millennial generation. For communication scholars it is important to not only think about what we say, but how we say it. Arguing that we have not yet successfully determined how to effectively communicate with younger audiences, Shulman details how communication interventions can help bolster the civic perceptions and engagement of Millennials by highlighting three root causes of civic disengagement: motivation, abilities, and opportunity. She examines each cause in turn, identifying potential "interventions" for each source of disengagement. On motivation, Shulman explores the connection between positive political social norms on a college campus and the resulting political behavior of that campus.

Testing whether normative perceptions can act as a motivator for civic engagement, she finds that cultivating a supportive normative environment contributes to political participation. Her research on abilities examines the impact of political group discussions and accessible language and how they can translate into improved political abilities. When it comes to enhancing opportunities for political engagement, Shulman argues that increased frequency of political communication can lead to greater political participation.

Shulman's chapter stands as a useful contrast to the other chapters that fall exclusively within the field of political science. Reinforcing a communication-centric approach, Shulman highlights the importance of carefully thinking about how we try to engage the Millennial generation. Greater emphasis needs to be placed on how we talk about politics because the incorporation of specific communication tactics can dramatically increase political engagement.

In chapter 4, Stephen M. Caliendo, Suzanne M. Chod, William J. Muck, and Deron Schreck narrow the discussion further to explore one particular type of Web 2.0 technology, Twitter. They investigate whether when used in an open and dynamic college classroom, Twitter can help students become more civically engaged. Along with Facebook, Twitter has emerged as a primary social media source for acquiring news. Because of its dynamic format, Twitter allows its users to easily find, share and debate political news. For students interested in the political world, Twitter appears an ideal technology for promoting students' political knowledge and civic engagement. After discussing their own experiences with using Twitter in Introduction to American Government courses, the authors offer results of an experimental design using students in multiple sections of an Introduction to Political Science course. Using a pre/posttest design to measure political interest, internal efficacy, and external efficacy, they find that while students were significantly more efficacious and reported higher levels of political interest at the end of the course, those differences were not the result of using Twitter.

The authors acknowledge that these sobering findings provide an important opportunity to reflect on the challenges of using technology in the classroom to promote civic engagement. The findings suggest that Twitter does not independently foster civic engagement in the classroom. Yet the authors are quick to note that there are many other benefits to using Twitter, including students' enjoyment using it in class and the additional engagement it offers to the instructor. We must think more deeply about the specific ways faculty use technology in the classroom and develop assessments consistent with those methods.

The final chapter examines the other dominant contemporary social media platform, Facebook. Leah A. Murray undertakes a comparative analysis of Facebook in two introductory American government courses. In one course she employs a conventional discussion board for the class's current event assignment, and in the other, students used Facebook for discussion. The author hypothesizes that students' comfort and familiarity with Facebook will make them more likely to engage in political discourse than a traditional discussion board. However, as in previous chapters, Murray finds mixed evidence. Students who used Facebook did generate more political knowledge, but the lack of difference on measures of civic engagement parallels the findings of previous chapters.

Separate from the findings on civic engagement, Murray notes that the use of Facebook fosters a dramatically more robust classroom experience because it creates a virtual water cooler where students willfully congregate to discuss current events. Moreover, like the Caliendo, Chod, Muck, and Schreck chapter on Twitter, the students report enjoying the experience of using Facebook in the classroom. This is significant in that for both the Twitter and Facebook studies, students enjoy using technology in the classroom, not unlike the Shulman chapter which emphasizes that providing a supportive and accessible environment is an important first step for promoting civic engagement. Yet, also like the other chapters, Murray reminds us of the complex process of unpacking technology's impact on the classroom.

As a whole, the chapters in this edition explore the intersection of the traditional classroom with the broad array of online technologies now available to faculty and students. The approaches and technologies examined are innovative and varied, but a common connection between all of the offerings is the question of how and in what specific ways the incorporation of technology into the college classroom can foster student civic engagement. The chapters also demonstrate the degree to which this field of inquiry is in very early stages. Many of the studies in this edition are the first of their kind. Consequently, the chapters in this edition stand as an opening statement in what we hope will become a rigorous discussion within a field of scholarly inquiry.

References

APSA Task Force on Civic Education in the 21st Century. 1998. "Expanded Articulation Statement: A Call for Reactions and Contributions." *PS: Political Science and Politics* 31 (September): 636–637.

Astin, Alexander W. and Linda J. Sax. 1998. "How Undergraduates Are Affected by Service Participation." *Journal of College Student Development* 39 (May/June): 251–263.

Bennett, Daniel and Pam Fielding. 1999. *The Net Effect: How Cyberadvocacy Is Changing the Political Landscape*. Merrifield, VA: e-Advocates Press.

Bimber, Bruce. 2001. "Information and Political Engagement in America: The Search for Effects of Information Technology at the Individual Level." *Political Research Quarterly* 54 (March): 53–67.

Birge, James, Brooke Beaird, and Jan Torres. 2003. "Partnerships among Colleges and Universities for Service Learning." In *Building Partnerships for Service-Learning*, edited by Barbara Jacoby. San Francisco: Jossey-Bass, 131–150.

Browning, Graeme. 1996. *Electronic Democracy: Using the Internet to Influence Politics*. Wilton, CT: Online Inc.

Bukovchik, VanVechten Renée, and Anita Chadha. 2013. "How Students Talk to Each Other: An Academic Social Networking

Project." In *Teaching Civic Engagement: From Student to Active Citizen*, edited by Alison Rios Millett McCartney, Elizabeth A. Bennison, and Dick Simpson. Washington, DC: American Political Science Association.

Campbell, David E. 2008. "Voice in the Classroom: How an Open Classroom Climate Fosters Political Engagement Among Adolescents." *Political Behavior* 30 (December): 437–454.

Carpenter, Charli and Daniel W. Drezner. 2010. "International Relations 2.0: The Implications of New Media for an Old Profession." *International Studies Perspectives* 11 (August): 255–272.

Dertouzos, Michael. 1997. *What Will Be: How the New Information Marketplace Will Change Our Lives.* San Francisco: Harper.

Delli Carpini, Michael X. 2000. "Gen.com: Youth, Civic Engagement, and the New Information Environment." *Political Communication* 17 (4): 341–349.

Eikenberry, Angela A. 2012. "Social Networking, Learning, and Civic Engagement: New Relationships between Professors and Students, Public Administrators and Citizens." *Journal of Public Affairs Education* 18(Summer): 449–466.

Ellison, Nicole B., Charles Steinfeld, and Cliff Lampe. 2007. "The Benefits of Facebook 'Friends': Social Capital and College Students' Use of Online Social Network Sites." *Journal of Computer-Mediated Communication* 12 (July): 1143–1168.

Galston, William A. 2004. "Civic Education and Political Participation." *PS: Political Science and Politics* 2 (April): 263–266.

Galston, William A. 2007. "Civic Knowledge, Civic Education, and Civic Engagement: A Summary of Recent Research." *International Journal of Public Administration* 30 (February): 623–642.

Gil de Zúñiga, Homero, Nakwon Jung, and Sebastián Valenzuela. 2012. "Social Media Use for News and Individuals' Social Capital, Civic Engagement and Political Participation." *Journal of Computer-Mediated Communication* 17 (April): 319–336.

Greenhow, Christine and Bejamin Gleason. 2012. "Twitteracy: Tweeting as a New Literacy Practice." *The Educational Forum* 76: 463–477.

Grossman, Lawrence K. 1995. *The Electronic Republic: Reshaping Democracy in America.* New York: Viking.

Hibbing, John R., and Elizabeth Theiss-Morse. 1996. "Civics is Not Enough: Teaching Barbarics in K-12." *PS: Political Science and Politics* 29 (March): 57–62.

Hunter, Susan and Richard A. Brisbin, Jr. 2000. "The Impact of Service Learning on Democratic and Civic Values." *PS: Political Science and Politics* 33 (September): 623–626.

Johnson, Thomas J. and Barbara E. Kaye. 1998. "A Vehicle for Engagement or a Haven for the Disaffected? Internet Use, Political Alienation, and Voter Participation." *In Engaging the Public: How Government and the Media Can Reinvigorate American Democracy*, edited by Thomas J. Johnson, Carol E. Hays, and Scott P. Hays. New York: Rowman & Littlefield, 123–135.

Junco, Reynol, Greg Heiberger, and Eric Loken. 2011. "The Effect of Twitter on College Student Engagement and Grades." *Journal of Computer Assisted Learning* 27 (April): 119–132.

Katz, James E. and Ronald E. Rice. 2002. *Social Consequences of Internet Use: Access, Involvement, and Interaction*. Cambridge: MIT Press

Lampe, Cliff, Nicole B. Ellison, and Charles Steinfield. 2006. "A Face(book) in the Crowd: Social Searching vs. Social Browsing." Presented at the 20th Anniversary Conference on Computer Supported Cooperative Work, Alberta, Canada. https://www.msu.edu/~nellison/lampe_et_al_2006.pdf (February 19, 2015).

Levine, Peter and Mark Hugo Lopez. 2002. "Youth Voting Has Declined, by Any Measure." September. http://civicyouth.org/research/products/Measuring_Youth_Voter_Turnout.pdf (February 19, 2015).

Levine, Peter. 2007. *The Future of Democracy: Developing the Next Generation of American Citizens*. Lebanon, NH: University Press of New England

McCartney, Allison Rios Millet. 2006. "Making the World Real: Using a Civic Engagement Course to Bring Home Our Global Connections." *Journal of Political Science Education* 2 (January): 113–128.

Miller, William E. and J. Merrill Shanks. 1996. *The New American Voter*. Cambridge: Harvard University Press.

Morris, Dick. 2000. *Vote.com*. Los Angeles: Renaissance Books.

Negroponte, Nicholas. 1995. *Being Digital*. New York: Knopf.

Newcomb, Theodore Mead, Katheryne E. Koenig, Richard Flacks, and Donald P. Warwick. 1967. *Persistence and Change: Bennington College and Its Students after Twenty-Five Years*. New York: John Wiley and Sons.

Niemi, Richard G. and M. Kent Jennings. 1991. "Issues and Inheritance in the Formation of Party Identification." *American Journal of Political Science* 35 (November): 970–988.

Niemi, Richard G. and Jane Junn. 1998. *Civic Education: What Makes Students Learn*. New Haven. CT: Yale University Press.

Norris, Pippa. 1999. "Who Surfs? New Technologies, Old Voters and Virtual Democracy." In *Democracy.com Governance in a Networked World*, edited by Elaine C. Kamarck and Joseph S. Nye. Hollis, NH: Hollis Publishing, 45–62.

Norris, Pippa. 2001. *Digital Divide? Civic Engagement, Information Poverty and the Internet Worldwide.* Cambridge: Cambridge University Press.

Pasek, Josh, Eian More, and Daniel Romer. 2009. "Realizing the Social Internet? Online Social Networking Meets Offline Civic Engagement. *Journal of Information Technology & Politics* 6 (July): 197–215.

Perry, James L. and Michael C. Katula. 2001. "Does Service Affect Citizenship? *Administration & Society* 33 (July): 330– 365

Prentice, Mary. 2007. "Service Learning and Civic Education." *Academic Questions* 20 (June): 135–145

Putnam, Robert D. 2000. *Bowling Alone: The Collapse and Revival of American Community.* New York: Simon and Schuster.

Spiezio, Kim E., Kerrie Q. Baker, and Kathleen Boland. 2005. "General Education and Civic Engagement: An Empirical Analysis of Pedagogical Possibilities." *JGE: The Journal of General Education* 54 (4): 273–292.

Steinfield, Charles, Nicole B. Ellison, and Cliff Lampe. 2008. "Social Capital, Self-Esteem, and Use of Online Social Network Sites: A Longitudinal Analysis." *Journal of Applied Developmental Psychology* 29 (November/December): 434–445.

Valenzuela, Sebastián, Namsu Park, and Kerk F. Kee. 2009. "Is There Social Capital in a Social Network Site?: Facebook Use and College Students' Life Satisfaction, Trust, and Participation." *Journal of Computer-Mediated Communication* 14 (July): 875–901.

Wattenberg Martin P. 2002. *Where Have All the Voters Gone?* Cambridge: Harvard University Press.

Yates, Miranda and James Youniss. 1996. "A Developmental Perspective on Community Service in Adolescence." *Social Development* 5 (March): 85–111.

CHAPTER 1

Taking College-Level Political Science Courses and Civic Activity

Kenneth W. Moffett and Laurie L. Rice

INTRODUCTION

The annual Cooperative Institutional Research Program Freshman Survey (2013) showed a 40 percent decrease in the number of incoming college freshmen who think that keeping up with politics is important. In 1966, 60 percent of this group thought that keeping up with politics was important (Galston 2004), while only 36.1 percent thought so in 2013 (Eagan et al. 2013). This trend coincides with research findings that indicate that the percentage of young adults who exercise suffrage has declined in this timeframe (Levine and Lopez 2002; Miller and Shanks 1996), and that young adults are less apt than their elders to engage in other forms of political activity such as contributing money to political parties or candidates, contacting their elected officials, or voting (Rosenstone and Hansen 1993; Zukin et al. 2006).

Surprisingly, these trends occur as an increasing number of American states require some form of civic education prior to high school graduation. In fact, 45 states and the District of Columbia currently require that high school students complete a course in American government or civics prior to graduation

(Center for Information and Research on Civic Learning and Engagement [CIRCLE] 2014).[1] Several researchers have investigated whether these courses lead to higher levels of subsequent civic activity, with earlier studies furnishing little evidence that taking these courses has a positive effect (Langton and Jennings 1968), but later studies suggesting a strong, positive effect on civic engagement after having taken such a class (Campbell 2008; Feldman et al. 2007; Kahne and Sporte 2008; Niemi and Junn 1998).

The more recent set of results implies that civic education leads to higher levels of civic activity in later life stages, regardless of when this education takes place. Yet, this proposition has not been fully explored, since there is little research that examines whether taking such a course as part of a student's undergraduate education has the same effect. We have reason to explore this proposition, as Flanagan and Levine (2010, 159) emphatically state that colleges have become "the central institution for civic incorporation of younger generations." In the present chapter, we explore this proposition and argue that taking a course in political science, civics, or American government at the college or university level positively affects civic activity. To test this argument, we begin by discussing why political science courses matter and how they might affect civic activity. Then, we discuss a variety of other factors that also affect civic engagement. We use a survey of undergraduate students at Southern Illinois University Edwardsville to test our theoretical expectations. Finally, we discuss our results and their implications for encouraging the civic activity of college students.

IMPORTANCE OF CIVIC ACTIVITY AND EDUCATION

Aristotle (350 BC) stated that the survival of a polity partly depends on an engaged citizenry. To foster this citizenry in the context of the appropriate constitution of the state, politicians must create institutions, including a system of moral education to frame this document for the citizenry (Aristotle 350 BC). He argued that this education should consist of training the young in the spirit of the constitution, including their responsibilities as members of society (Aristotle 350 BC, Book Five). These responsibilities included participating in the Athenian assembly or council, as well as serving on juries (Aristotle 350 BC).

By engaging in these and other similar activities, citizens collectively articulate the general will of society at large (Rousseau 1762). To effectively enact this will, Rousseau (1762) argues that it is vital that citizens regularly participate in assemblies and other routes by which to express preferences between alternatives. Dahl (1991) extends this argument and states that one of the defining characteristics of a democracy is that each citizen performs acts that constitute expressing preferences over alternatives on a regular basis. However, elected officeholders are responsible for enacting policies that reflect the preferences of the public at large (Dahl 1991, 2006). At the same time, these officeholders cannot do so unless citizens actively articulate their preferences.

To state their preferences, citizens must be sufficiently educated so that they can meaningfully differentiate between candidates and between complex policy alternatives. In his farewell address, former president George Washington (1796) noted the importance of civic education and said that "it is essential that public opinion should be enlightened." Former president Thomas Jefferson (1903, 278) expressed similar sentiments when he stated that, in governing, the population should "inform their discretion by education."

In this spirit, Congress requires American schoolchildren to be tested periodically for proficiency in civics (Gibson and Levine 2003, 5). Also, most state governments mandate some form of education about civics, government, or politics prior to graduating with a high school diploma (CIRCLE 2014). At least one state, Texas, requires all graduates of public colleges and universities to take at least six semester credit hours in government or political science (The University of Texas 2014). In addition, all students who receive an undergraduate degree from the California State University system are also mandated to have taken one course in American government and California politics (California State University System 2014).

While there is a seemingly clear philosophical, normative, historical, and material commitment to civic education, one should ask whether these courses succeed in fostering an increased level of civic activity. Niemi and Junn (1998) discovered that civic education at the primary and secondary education levels increased political knowledge among high school students by approximately 4 percent. Moreover, Kahne and Westheimer (2006) found that civic education at these levels increased levels of internal efficacy among students, but does relatively little to change external efficacy. In addition, Gainous and Martens (2012) discovered that civic education at the primary and secondary levels helps students when instructors employ a variety of instructional methods. In particular, civic education at these levels assists those students from less-privileged backgrounds the most (Gainous and Martens 2012).

While these studies help make a prima facie case that civic education matters at the primary and secondary educational levels, they only examine the effects of such education at these levels. As a consequence, the conclusions from these studies might not extend beyond the scope to which they were confined. After all, primary and secondary education through 12th grade is mandated, in some form, in all 50 states. Moreover, civic education is mandated in some form in 45 out of 50 states (CIRCLE 2014). In addition, the vast majority of this instruction occurs before students are eligible to vote.

In contrast, college-level civic education is aimed at students who have already obtained the rights and responsibilities that come with reaching the pivotal age of 18. This makes investigating the effects of civic education at the college level particularly important to extending our knowledge about civic education. Colleges and universities have a unique role in American society, since an increasing percentage of the population is successfully completing undergraduate education. During their time in college, many students are continuing the process of becoming fully mature adults and are forming opinions about a wide variety of matters, including politics. Consequently, students who take at least one course in government and politics might be spurred to civic activity in ways that they otherwise would not have. For these reasons, it makes sense to examine whether taking political science courses at the college level affects civic activity.

POLITICAL SCIENCE COURSES AND CIVIC ENGAGEMENT

Political science, government, or civics courses might enhance civic activity because of the nature of the subject matter. More specifically, students who take these courses increase their knowledge about politics, typically discuss politics as part of the course, and can be assigned tasks that require engagement with the political process. These courses can also be integrative in the sense that they tie together other, seemingly unrelated courses in a way that fosters higher levels of civic activity than would have occurred in the absence of having taken the course.

Students who take courses that primarily examine government, politics, or civics learn basic facts about politics (Flanagan and Levine 2010). For example, many students who take an introductory American politics course learn about the Constitution, civil rights and liberties, political institutions, political behavior, and the public policymaking process. Consequently, these students acquire an awareness of core tenets that surround politics that might not have existed had they not taken the course (Niemi and Junn 1998). In addition, students who take these courses receive information that aids in forming opinions about politics. Consequently, these newly acquired opinions might encourage students to engage in civic activity for some timespan after having taken a political science course (Flanagan and Levine 2010).

Moreover, students who take political science courses are most likely exposed to an open classroom environment in political science courses that includes discussions about politics (Campbell 2008; Feldman et al. 2007; Klofstad 2015). These discussions build upon the knowledge that was, or is in the process of being acquired, and encourage interactions between students, instructors, and fellow classmates (Campbell 1998; Klofstad 2015; Oros 2007). Consequently, discussing politics within the context of a course might encourage students to reconsider long-held opinions, encourage the formations of new ones, and heighten the level of engagement with the material at the time that the class was taken (Campbell 1998; Feldman et al. 2007; Flanagan and Levine 2010; Klofstad 2015; Oros 2007). Thus, these discussions might facilitate higher levels of civic activity well after the course was taken (Klofstad 2015; Oros 2007).

Additionally, students who take courses in political science may be exposed to assignments or activities that require involvement that extends beyond taking exams and ordinary classroom participation. For instance, some introductory courses in American politics require students to register to vote, attend city council meetings, participate in a service-learning exercise, or even, attend federal court proceedings, (Flanagan and Levine 2010). Moreover, researchers have found that courses that have a simulation component to them yield higher levels of engagement during the semester, and higher levels of civic activity once the course is concluded (Feldman et al. 2007). Also, Flanagan and Levine (2010) argue that taking courses that contain a service-learning experience may increase engagement in civic life upon completion of these classes. In a similar vein, Gainous and Martens (2012) and Kahne and Sporte (2008) discover that students who take courses in civics taught

by instructors who utilize a wide range of instructional methods are more highly engaged, and have higher levels of efficacy. As a result, the nature of assignments in political science
courses might facilitate higher levels of civic engagement after
the course concludes.

Finally, political science courses might tie together other
seemingly disparate courses in which government or civics is
not the primary focus. For example, an elementary education
major who learns how to implement varying state and federal
requirements would learn the process by which these requirements were created in an introductory American politics course.
More generally, political science courses are a component of
many universities' general education requirements and can
nicely buttress and bring together politically relevant material
that is taught in one or more of the other courses. For these
reasons, we should expect that students who take political science courses are more likely to engage in civic activities than
those who do not take such classes.

We examine the relationship between taking political science
classes and engaging in four specific forms of civic engagement:
contacting government officials, contacting newspapers, participating in protests, and joining off-campus political groups.
These vary in the time and effort required, the number of people who engage in them, as well as the degree of linkage to
the typical political science class. Political science courses are
likely to emphasize the importance of elected officials hearing
from citizens as well as the influence that political groups can
have on election outcomes and public policy decisions. Further,
introductory American government classes that cover the civil
rights movement typically discuss how protests influenced public opinion and public policy. Students who have taken a political science class should be more likely to see the potential value
of each of these activities. Contacting newspapers may have the
least amount of linkage to course content as well as the lowest
familiarity to students.[2] Still, letters to the editor are a forum

of civic expression that get some attention in political science courses.

OTHER FACTORS THAT INFLUENCE CIVIC ENGAGEMENT

Beyond the impact of taking a political science course, researchers have found that other factors influence varying forms of civic engagement. Earlier, we suggested that the act of taking a political science course might act alongside other predictors in explaining political activity. In the proceeding paragraphs, we examine the roles that online activities, as well as respondent and political characteristics play, in fostering civic engagement.

Online Activities

The Internet has played a central role in the lives of today's college students. For example, today's college students were very young when blogs were invented in 1994 (Thompson 2006). Further, these same students grew up when blogs revealed a number of large-scale news items including the initial bit of information that surrounded then-president Clinton's relations with Monica Lewinsky in 1998, and then-senate majority leader Trent Lott's comments about Strom Thurmond in 2002 (Bloom 2003; Wallsten 2007). Moreover, many of these students were around for the inventions of social media platforms such as Myspace and LinkedIn in 2003, Facebook in 2004, and Twitter in 2006 (Curtiss 2014). Consequently, these students are much more likely to see online expression, whatever form that it may take, as a normal way to share information and opinions about a variety of topics, including politics.

Through Facebook and other similar websites, users can click a button that indicates that they like a particular comment, page, or person. Users can also click similar buttons or links to join groups, and become friends or followers of particular persons or groups. This may lead to requests for political participation. Numerous studies link engaging in one form of online political activity to engaging in other forms of political activity (see, e.g., Best and Kruger 2005; Lewis 2011; Towner and Dulio 2011; Towner 2013). For example, Rice, Moffett, and Madupalli (2013) found that college students were more likely to actively participate in other forms of political participation when they joined an online political social network, or friended a candidate or party. Consequently, we anticipate that those who engage in friending or joining activity via social networks are more likely to engage in a variety of civic activities.

Yet, online political expression that extends beyond friending requires more of a commitment than clicking a mouse button, or tapping "like" on a tablet. Online political expression can also take on a form that requires an individual to elaborate her or his thoughts for a wider audience to see and engage. Toward this end, Wellman et al. (2001, 450) predicted that people who participate online will become more active in offline political activities. Min (2007) discovered that online political expression positively affects how much people know about issues, levels of political efficacy, and especially, one's willingness to participate in politics. Similarly, Moffett and Rice (2014) found that college students are more likely to participate in other forms of offline political activities when they engaged in online political expression. Thus, we expect that those who engage in online political expression that extends beyond friending or joining activity are more likely to engage in a variety of civic activities. This may hold especially true for other forms of expressive activity.

There is some evidence that people are more likely to participate in civic activity when they are familiar with the mechanisms by which to do so. For example, Gil de Zuniga, Puig-I-Abril, and Rojas (2009) discovered that reading politically oriented blogs is connected with higher levels of participation in politics. This exposure to information about politics and people's opinions about it might encourage students to generate their own opinions and the desire to express those in a variety of ways. Further, prior research suggests that reading blogs about current events and politics might be connected with higher levels of political expression in other ways, especially online (see Kenski and Stroud 2006; Lewis 2011). As a result, we anticipate higher levels of engaging in civic activities among those who read politically oriented blogs.

Other research suggests that using the Internet in an informational way, such as reading news online, is connected with higher levels of political participation (Feldman et al. 2007; Kenski and Stroud 2006; Norris 1998; Shah, Kwak, and Holbert 2001; Shah et al. 2005; Tolbert and McNeal 2003). Consuming such news can spark the creative impetus to engage in civic activities, especially more expressive forms in which one articulates his or her opinions for a broader audience. Political news can also inform readers of opportunities to become involved in politics, such as upcoming campaign appearances, rallies, and other activities. Thus, we expect that those who spend more time consuming online news might be more apt to engage in higher levels of civic activities.

Respondent and Political Characteristics

We now turn our attention to examine the role that more conventional predictors of civic activity play. The extant research on civic activity suggests that other, more standard explanations of civic activity might help explain variance in civic activity. Below, we theorize how each of these factors operates when it comes to explaining the mechanisms that college students use to civically engage.

Students' level of civic activity may be influenced by that of their peers. More specifically, students whose friends are more civically engaged might participate at higher levels as a by-product of being socially networked with other highly engaged peers. Social networks are known to influence a wide variety of activities, including increased electoral engagement (McClurg

2003) and patterns of giving to political campaigns (Gimpel, Lee and Kamiski 2006). We expect the influence of peers to exert a strong impact on those activities that tend to be done collectively, such as participating in protests, but less of an effect, if any, among those activities that are more solitary in nature.

In addition, strength of partisanship acts as an effective predictor of most traditional forms of political activity (see e.g., Rosenstone and Hansen 1993; Verba, Schlozman, and Brady 1995). Those with stronger ties to one of the political parties tend to have stronger political views and are more highly interested in election outcomes. Seemingly, one might expect that strong partisans, regardless of age, might be expected to engage in higher levels of civic activity. Yet, strong attachments to political parties are not equally distributed across all age groups. More specifically, Dugan (2013) found that younger adults are more likely to self-identify as pure independents compared with older Americans. In this way, strong partisanship might not carry the same meaning to younger adults, as dissatisfaction with both political parties could also motivate civic activity in the same way as strongly identifying with one of the political parties. Consequently, we anticipate that those who strongly identify with one of the political parties may be no more likely to engage in civic activities than those who do not have such attachments.

Interest in politics strongly predicts political activity in most cases, as those who engage in a variety of civic activities have intrinsic motivators for doing so (Campbell et al. 1960; Rosenstone and Hansen 1993; Verba and Nie 1972; Verba, Schlozman, and Brady 1995). After all, why should one take the time to engage in civic activity if s/he is uninterested in politics? Yet, this interest might not have an equal effect across all forms of civic activity, since those that are more costly may require higher levels of interest in politics to encourage people to participate. If true, then we anticipate that interest in politics should be positively connected with participating in protests and joining political groups, rather than contacting newspapers or elected officials. Participating in protests and joining political groups require a higher level of commitment, both public and private, than one-time acts such as contacting newspapers or elected officials.

We also control for the effects of a student's choice of major, and opinions about President Obama's handling of the economy. Political science majors should be more knowledgeable about and interested in politics and will have taken more political science classes than those who decide to major in other subjects. This might lead to higher levels of civic activity, as opposed to nonpolitical science majors. Secondarily, those who major in social science majors that are connected with political science, such as economics or sociology, might be more likely to engage in civic activity than nonsocial science majors.

Finally, we also control for the effects of views on the economy on civic activity. Lewis-Beck (1990) and many others found that the state of the economy affects voting behavior around the world, including in the United States. Owing to the impact of the Great Recession, the economy affected younger Americans more than older ones, as those who graduated during this time were less likely to have secured jobs after graduation than those who came before them (Abel, Dietz, and Su 2014). In particular, younger college graduates are more likely to be underemployed in the jobs that they do occupy (Abel, Dietz, and Su 2014). Since the state of the economy has a unique, negative effect on younger Americans, dissatisfaction with the president's actions with respect to handling of the economy might affect patterns of civic activity.[3]

DATA AND METHODS

We performed web-based surveys of randomly chosen, full-time, undergraduate students between the ages of 18 and 25 at Southern Illinois University, Edwardsville, between October 16 and October 23, 2012. This university is a four-year, Masters-level university located approximately 20 miles from St. Louis, Missouri with approximately 14,000 students. We employed Internet-based instruments to investigate a variety of ways in which one can be civically engaged, including friending and joining activities and online political expression, because one cannot perform these activities when s/he lacks the ability to use a computer to complete basic tasks, like participating in this type of survey.

To execute our survey, we used the complete list of university-assigned student e-mail addresses to give each undergraduate an opportunity to participate. Around 626 of the 9,759 students who were eligible to complete the survey completed it. The response rate for this survey (6.4%) lies on the low end of response rates that others have reported for surveys conducted in this fashion (Thies and Hogan 2005). That said, others have recently faced higher levels of resistance to survey participation that have yielded declining response rates (see Pew 2012a). Additionally, this sample is fairly representative of the student population at this institution, and provides a 3.79 percent margin of error when we interpret the results.[4]

Three of our dependent variables asked about the frequency with which one contacted government officials, contacted newspapers to express views about politics, and participated in politically oriented protests. We asked each respondent to rate the frequency with which s/he has engaged in each activity on a five point scale that ranged from "never" to "very often." We employed an ordered logistic regression to test our expectations, since these dependent variables are ordered. The final dependent variable asked whether each respondent joined a politically oriented group away from a college campus. We used logistic regression to test our expectations with respect to this variable, since this variable is binary. Appendix B provides a more detailed discussion of the variables used in this analysis.

To measure our primary independent variable, we asked whether each respondent has taken a course on government, politics, or civic education. We expect a positive sign on this variable. Further, we employed four questions that asked participants about the frequency with which they engage in a variety of online activities. First, we asked each respondent how often s/he friended or joined a professional network related to a presidential candidate or political party on a social networking site. Second, we asked each respondent how frequently s/he expressed his or her views about politics online. Third, each student was asked how often s/he read Internet blogs about politics and current events. Fourth, we asked each student how frequently s/he read news on the Internet about politics and current events. The items that we used to measure these four concepts were answered on five-point response scales for which zero points were allocated to "Not at all," and four points for "Very often."

We employed two variables to investigate the effects of respondent characteristics on online engagement. To investigate the effects of peer civic experiences on a variety of civic activities, we constructed an index based on the replies that were given to three questions that examine the extent to which the friends of each student engaged in a series of activities. Each of the questions that we used to measure this concept were answered on a five-point response scale for which zero points were allocated to "strongly disagree," one point for "disagree," two points for "neutral," three points for "agree," and four points for "strongly agree" ($\alpha = 0.70$).[5]

Second, we consider strength of partisan attachment, since this predicts many forms of political activity (see, e.g., Rosenstone and Hansen 1993; Verba, Schlozman, and Brady 1995). To measure the degree of partisanship among respondents, each student was asked whether s/he identifies him or herself as a Democrat, Republican, independent, or something else. Using two questions with somewhat different wordings, each respondent who self-identified as a Republican or Democrat was asked whether s/he strongly or not strongly identified as a Republican or Democrat, respectively. We constructed a dichotomous variable that is coded one for strong partisans from this set of questions.

We employed five variables to investigate the effects of political characteristics. First, we asked each student about the extent to which s/he is interested in politics. We used a four-point scale for this question, where three points were allocated to "Very Interested," two points for "Somewhat Interested," one point for "Not Very Interested," and zero points for "Not at all Interested."[6] Second, we asked each student to identify his or her major(s). From here, we constructed two binary variables: one for political science majors, and the other for those who majored in a social science discipline *other than* political science. The comparison category for both variables consists of those students who majored in a discipline other than social science.

Finally, we considered the effect of political issues on online engagement by asking how students felt about President Obama's handling of the economy. From the questions about this subject, we generated two binary variables: one for those who disapproved of the president's handling of the economy, and the other for those who strongly disapproved of his handling of the economy. The comparison category for both variables consists of those who approve to any degree of the way in which the president has handled the economy, or responded that they did not know whether they approve or disapprove.[7]

Results

Table 1.1 displays the results. The first model uses contacting government officials as the dependent variable. Model Two employs contacting newspapers about politics as the response variable. Model Three uses participating in protests as the

Table 1.1 Civic activities and political science course enrollment

Independent variable	Contact government officials	Contact newspapers	Participate in protests	Join political group	Join political group (predicted probabilities)
Taking a political science course	0.506*	0.816*	0.574*	0.912*	0.071*
	(0.264)	(0.431)	(0.324)	(0.458)	(0.038)
Online activities					
Friending and joining	0.242*	0.518***	0.143	−0.011	0.003
	(0.106)	(0.157)	(0.126)	(0.154)	(0.019)
Online political expression	0.178*	0.242	0.323**	0.233	0.033
	(0.103)	(0.156)	(0.121)	(0.143)	(0.028)
Online news reading	0.128	−0.680**	−0.486**	0.052	0.009
	(0.136)	(0.234)	(0.174)	(0.220)	(0.031)
Political blog reading	−0.139	0.416*	0.278*	0.104	0.015
	(0.105)	(0.186)	(0.130)	(0.146)	(0.022)
Respondent characteristics					
Peer civic experiences	0.100*	0.036	0.176**	0.090	0.014
	(0.051)	(0.078)	(0.063)	(0.074)	(0.014)
Strong partisan	−0.406	−0.582	−0.194	−0.272	−0.013
	(0.271)	(0.420)	(0.316)	(0.388)	(0.021)
Political characteristics					
Interest in politics	0.218	−0.011	0.563*	0.747*	0.062*
	(0.206)	(0.311)	(0.254)	(0.337)	(0.043)
Political science major	1.286**	0.934	0.752	1.216**	0.129**
	(0.437)	(0.618)	(0.468)	(0.511)	(0.091)
Other social science major	−0.306	−1.035	−0.670	0.114	0.010
	(0.357)	(0.663)	(0.457)	(0.475)	(0.033)
Disapprove of Obama's handling of the economy	−0.844*	0.223	−1.179*	−0.887	−0.030
	(0.438)	(0.513)	(0.587)	(0.689)	(0.028)
Strongly disapprove of Obama's handling of the economy	−0.057	−0.447	−0.385	−0.497	−0.022
	(0.250)	(0.401)	(0.297)	(0.378)	(0.021)
Cut point one	2.704***	2.594**	3.747***	–	–
	(0.559)	(0.802)	(0.699)		
Cut point two	3.607***	3.551***	4.654***	–	–
	(0.574)	(0.825)	(0.719)		
Cut point three	5.032***	4.848***	5.586***	–	–
	(0.621)	(0.906)	(0.751)		
Cut point four	5.940***	6.027***	6.581***	–	–
	(0.678)	(1.084)	(0.809)		
Constant	–	–	–	−5.415***	–
				(1.012)	
N	366	368	369	369	–
Log likelihood	−329.24	−152.55	−244.67	−112.49	–
Pseudo R^2	0.081	0.130	0.129	0.189	–
Chi-Square	58.22	45.41	72.34	52.58	–
Prob>Chi-Squared	<.0001	<.0001	<.0001	<0.0001	–
Percent correctly predicted	–	–	–	88.62%	–
Proportional reduction of error	–	–	–	0.087	–

Notes: First, the coefficients for contacting government, contacting newspapers, and participating in protests are ordered logit coefficients while the coefficients for joining an on-campus political group are logit coefficients. Second, the values in parenthesis are standard errors. Third, * denotes $p < 0.05$, ** denotes $p < 0.01$, and *** denotes $p < 0.0001$; all one-tailed tests.

dependent variable. Since the coefficient estimates for these models are not straightforward in terms of interpretation, we used odds ratios to interpret these coefficients. These ratios provide the ability to evaluate the impact that each coefficient has on our dependent variable in a more direct way than predicted probabilities can when using ordered logistic regression.[8]

Model Four uses joining political groups as the response variable. Since the coefficient estimates for Model Four do not lend themselves to being interpreted in a straightforward fashion, we used CLARIFY to compute the change in the predicted probabilities (King, Tomz, and Wittenberg 2000).[9] For Model Four, the predicted probabilities are displayed in the last column.

Online activities affect a variety of routes by which students civically engage. Overall, students who friend candidates or parties and join groups on Facebook, LinkedIn, or other social networking websites are more likely to contact government officials and contact newspapers. More specifically, the odds that favor higher levels of contacting government officials increase by 27.38 percent for each unit increase in friending or joining activity. In addition, the odds that favor higher levels of contacting newspapers increase by 67.87 percent for each unit increase in friending or joining activity.

Students who engage in online political expression are also more likely to contact government officials and participate in political protests. The odds that favor higher levels of contacting government officials increase by 19.48 percent for each unit increase in online political expression. Also, the odds that favor higher levels of participating in politically oriented protests increase by 38.13 percent for each unit increase in online political activity.

Respondents who engage in reading online news are less likely to contact newspapers and participate in protests. Each unit increase in online news readership decreases the odds that favor higher levels of contacting newspapers by 49.34 percent, and participating in protests by 38.49 percent. Yet, students who read political blogs are more likely to contact newspapers and participate in protests. More specifically, each unit increase in political blog reading increases the odds that favor higher levels of contacting newspapers by 51.59 percent, and participating in protests by 32.05 percent.

Yet, there is limited evidence that respondent characteristics drove civic activities. On the one hand, we discovered no evidence that being a strong partisan affected the propensity with which students contacted government officials, contacted newspapers, participated in protests, or joined political groups. That said, we found that each unit increase in the civic experiences of a student's peers increased the odds that favored higher levels of participating in protests by 19.24 percent, and higher levels of contacting government officials by 10.52 percent. Beyond this, there is no evidence that the experiences of a student's peers is connected with higher levels of specified civic activities.

Yet, there is some evidence that political characteristics are connected with changes in civic activity. We discovered that each unit increase in interest in politics increases the odds that one participated in political protests by 75.59 percent, and the probability that one joins a political group by 6.20 percent. Further, we found that being a political science major increases the odds that favor contacting government officials by 261.83 percent, and the probability that a student joins a political group by 12.90 percent. Interestingly, though, those who disapprove of President Obama's handling of the economy were less apt to contact government officials and participate in protests. More specifically, the odds that favored higher levels of contacting government officials decreased by 57 percent among respondents who disapproved of President Obama's handling of the economy. Additionally, the odds that favored higher levels of participating in politically oriented protests decreased by 69.24 percent among students who disapproved of President Obama's handling of the economy. Finally, we discovered no evidence that majoring in another social science discipline or strongly disapproving of Obama's handling of the economy is connected with a variety of specified civic activities.

Political Science Courses and Civic Engagement

Most importantly, we unearth substantial evidence that taking a political science course is connected with higher levels of contacting government officials, contacting newspapers, participating in protests, and joining political groups. To perform a more precise analysis of the results, we used CLARIFY to compute the change in the predicted probability of each form of civic activity when a student has taken a political science course while holding all other binary variables at zero and the values of all continuous variables at their means (King, Tomz, and Wittenberg 2000). In other words, we estimate the impact of taking a political science course among students who are not majoring in political science or another social science, are not strong partisans, either approve of Obama's handling of the economy to some extent or don't know their opinion, but exhibit mean levels of friending and joining activity, online political expression, online news reading, political blog reading, peer civic experiences, and interest in politics. In each figure, the vertical axis is the change in the predicted probability, and the horizontal axis is the frequency of each form of civic activity.

As Figure 1.1 shows, taking a political science course decreased the probability that a student never contacted officials by 10.95 percent. Yet, taking a course in political science increased the probabilities that a student rarely contacted government officials by 4.05 percent, sometimes contacts those officials by 4.65 percent, regularly contacts those officials by 1.27 percent, and contacts those officials very often by 1 percent. Figure 1.2 demonstrates that taking a political science course decreased the probability that a respondent never contacted newspapers by 7.62 percent,

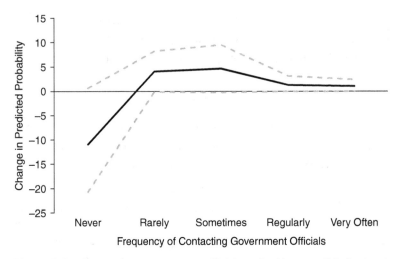

Figure 1.1 Contacting government officials and taking a political science course.

Notes: We used CLARIFY to compute change in the predicted probability of each level of contacting government officials (King, Tomz, and Wittenberg 2000). To compute this change, we assumed that all binary variables have a value of zero, and the values of all continuous variables are held at their mean. Then, we changed the value of taking a political science course from zero to one. Finally, the solid line denotes the mean change in predicted probability, while the dashed line denotes the 95 percent confidence interval surrounding this predicted change.

but increased the probabilities that a student rarely contacted newspapers by 4.14 percent, sometimes contacted newspapers by 2.42 percent, regularly contacted newspapers by .7 percent, and contacted newspapers very often by 0.4 percent. Figure 1.3 illustrates that taking a course in political science decreased the probability that a student never participated in a politically oriented protest by 9.48 percent, but increased the probabilities that a respondent rarely participated in this activity by 4.35 percent, sometimes participated in this activity by 2.80 percent, regularly participated in this activity by 1.38 percent, and participated in this activity very often by 1 percent. Finally, the probability that a student joins a political group away from a college campus increases by 7.1 percent when s/he took a political science course.

We verified whether the results were an artifact of the way in which the models were specified. To check this, we

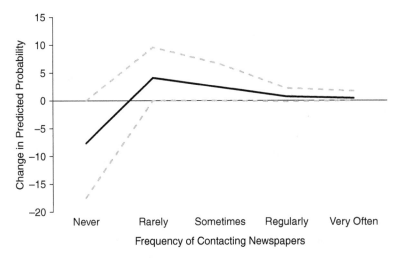

Figure 1.2   Contacting newspapers and taking a political science course.

Notes: We used CLARIFY to compute change in the predicted probability of each level of contacting newspapers (King, Tomz, and Wittenberg 2000). To compute this change, we assumed that all binary variables have a value of zero, and the values of all continuous variables are held at their mean. Then, we changed the value of taking a political science course from zero to one. Finally, the solid line denotes the mean change in predicted probability, while the dashed line denotes the 95 percent confidence interval surrounding this predicted change.

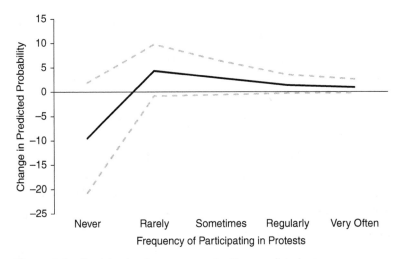

Figure 1.3   Participating in protests and taking a political science course.

Notes: We used CLARIFY to compute change in the predicted probability of each level of participating in protests (King, Tomz, and Wittenberg 2000). To compute this change, we assumed that all binary variables have a value of zero, and the values of all continuous variables are held at their mean. Then, we changed the value of taking a political science course from zero to one. Finally, the solid line denotes the mean change in predicted probability, while the dashed line denotes the 95 percent confidence interval surrounding this predicted change.

removed one variable at a time and found that the results do not change in most specifications. Moreover, the overall statistics for each of the models indicate that knowing the values of the independent variables is useful in predicting our dependent variables. When we examine the joining model, 88.62 percent of cases are correctly predicted by the independent variables, and we reduce our error in predicting who joins political groups by 8.7 percent when we know the values of the independent variables.

CONCLUSION

To conclude, we found that students who take political science courses are more likely to contact newspapers, contact government officials, participate in protests, and join politically oriented groups. This finding is significant because it extends the research that examines the effectiveness of political science courses at fostering civic activity beyond the primary and secondary educational levels. In addition, our discovery encompasses a wide variety of ways by which students can civically act, including those that are seemingly solitary, such as contacting newspapers and government officials, and those that are of a more collective nature, like participating in protests and joining politically oriented groups.

In this vein, this study fits neatly within the larger literature that examines the effects of civic education on engagement in civic life. For example, this study comes to conclusions that are consistent with other findings that these courses increase civic activity (Campbell 2008; Flanagan and Levine 2010; Galston 2001; Niemi and Junn 1998). More specifically, our findings build upon previous research in that we find evidence that confirms the positive effect of political science courses in a way that extends beyond acquiring additional political knowledge, or curriculum-based community service requirements in a broader sense. In addition, the findings from this study concur with the broader research that emphasizes the activities that occur within the classroom environment over the mere act of receiving a civic education (see Campbell 2008; Feldman et al. 2007; Gainous and Martens 2012).

That said, the findings in this research come with at least two opportunities for other researchers to build upon our work. First, we only examined students at a single institution to observe the effects of political science courses on civic activity. This artifact is particularly significant, since students at this institution are *not* mandated to take any political science courses as a condition of graduating with their baccalaureate degree. That said, this concern might not be problematic, since students at the great majority of colleges and universities around the United States are similarly situated. In this vein, we are confident that the results obtained are not the product of students who are already more interested or engaged in politics making the decision to enroll in political science courses. Moreover, we have no reason to believe that students at this institution are atypical of the general population of college students around the United States. Thus, we are fairly confident that the results from this chapter can be generalized to the broader population of college students.

Second, we only examined the effects that taking a college course in political science have on civic activity. We did not investigate whether any of the specific activities that occur within political science courses, or courses in other disciplines, affect civic activity. It is entirely possible, and quite probable that activities such as discussing politics during scheduled class time, participation in simulations, and involvement in service-learning activities in political science courses have an equal, if not greater, impact on civic activity over the short- and long-term. However, this research has demonstrated that taking a political science course at the college-level positively affects the propensity to engage in a wide variety of civic activities. In this way, this study provides the logical foundation for future research to take the next step and learn what it is about political science courses, and courses in other disciplines that leads to the effects that we discovered in this analysis. Meanwhile, the results suggest that those interested in fostering the civic education of college students should encourage them to take a political science class.

Appendix A:Summary Statistics for Political Science Course Variables

Table 1.2   Summary statistics for political science course variables

Variable	Number of observations	Mean	Standard deviation	Minimum	Maximum
Contact government officials	619	0.504	0.932	0	4
Contact newspapers	623	0.177	0.582	0	4
Participate in protests		0.352	0.838	0	4
Join political group	627	0.099	0.299	0	1
Taking a political science course	627	0.583	0.494	0	1
Friending and joining activity	575	0.934	1.248	0	4
Online political expression	578	1.128	1.285	0	4
Online news reading	618	2.285	1.259	0	4
Political blog reading	620	1.426	1.332	0	4
Peer civic experiences	546	7.158	2.480	0	12
Strong partisan	626	0.321	0.467	0	1
Interest in politics	621	1.786	0.864	0	3
Political science major	617	0.055	0.228	0	1
Other social science major	617	0.120	0.325	0	1
Disapprove of Obama's handling of the economy	473	0.125	0.331	0	1
Strongly disapprove of Obama's handling of the economy	473	0.419	0.494	0	1

Appendix B: Question Wording for Variables

DEPENDENT VARIABLES

During 2012, how often have you . . .

Table 1.3 Frequency of government contact, media contact, and participation in Marches or other similar political activities

	Never				*Frequently*	*Don't know*
Contacted or visited someone in government who represents your community	0	1	2	3	4	DK
Contacted a newspaper, radio, or TV talk show to express your opinion on an issue	0	1	2	3	4	DK
Participated in political activities such as protests, marches, or demonstrations	0	1	2	3	4	DK

Have you ever joined a group or organization that deals with government or political issues beyond your university?
 1) Yes; 2) No; 3) Don't Know

INDEPENDENT VARIABLES

Taken a Political Science Course

At a college or university, have you taken a class on government, politics, or civic education?
 1) Yes; 2) No; 3) Don't Know

Friending and Joining Activity

During 2012, how often have you friended or joined a professional network related to a presidential candidate or political party on a social networking site such as Facebook or LinkedIn?

1) Never; 2) Rarely; 3) Sometimes; 4) Regularly; 5) Very Often

Online Political Expression

During 2012, how often have you expressed your views about politics on a website, blog, or chatroom?

1) Never; 2) Rarely; 3) Sometimes; 4) Regularly; 5) Very Often

Frequency of Online News Reading

In a typical week, how often do you read news on the Internet about politics and current events?

0) Not at All; 1) Rarely; 2) Sometimes; 3) Often; 4) Very Often; 5) Don't Know

Frequency of Political Blog Reading

In a typical week, how often do you read internet blogs about politics and current events?

0) Not at All; 1) Rarely; 2) Sometimes; 3) Often; 4) Very Often; 5) Don't Know

Peer Civic Experiences

Defined in the text.

Table 1.4 Correlation matrix among items in the peer civic experiences index

	Friends are active in volunteer work	Friends vote in elections	Friends encourage expression about politics and current events
Friends are active in volunteer work	1.000		
Friends vote in elections	0.410	1.000	
Friends encourage expression about politics and current events	0.315	0.5739	1.000

Strong Partisan

Generally speaking, do you usually think of yourself as a Republican, a Democrat, an Independent, or something else?

1) Republican; 2) Democrat; 3) Independent; 4) Other

If the respondent answered "Republican," for partisan identification, then s/he was asked the following question:

Do you think of yourself as strongly Republican or not very strong?

1) Strong Republican; 2) Not very strong Republican

If the respondent answered "Democrat," for partisan identification, then s/he was asked the following question:

Do you think of yourself as strongly Democratic or not very strong?

1) Strong Democrat; 2) Not very strong Democrat

Interest in Politics

How interested would you say you are in politics? Are you ...

0) Not at all interested; 1) Not very interested; 2) Somewhat interested; 3) Very interested; 4) Don't Know

Political Science and Other Social Science Major

If you have declared a major(s), what is your area(s) of study? (check all that apply)

_____ Arts; _____ Architecture ; _____ Business; _____ Education; _____ Engineering; _____ Humanities; _____ Interdisciplinary; _____ Math and Sciences; _____ Nursing; _____ Political Science; _____ Social Sciences, other than Political Science; _____ Social Work; _____ Undeclared; _____ Other

Disapproval of the President's Handling of the Economy

Do you approve or disapprove of the way that Barack Obama is handling the economy?

1) Approve; 2) Disapprove; 3) Don't Know

Strong Disapproval of the President's Handling of the Economy

If the respondent disapproved of the way that Barack Obama is handling the economy, then s/he was asked the following question:

How strongly do you disapprove of the way that Barack Obama is handling the economy?

1) Strongly; 2) Not Strongly

NOTES

1. The states that do not require courses in civics or American government as a graduation requirement are Alaska, Delaware, Montana, Oregon, and Rhode Island (Center for Information and Research on Civic Learning and Engagement 2014).
2. In 2012, a Pew Research Center survey showed only 6 percent of 18–24-year-olds nationwide said they got news from a print newspaper the previous day (Pew 2012b).
3. We chose to focus on the economy as the sole issue that is examined in this chapter because the economy was one of the major issues in the 2012 elections. In 2012, 90.32 percent of respondents responded that the economy was extremely or

very important. By contrast, only 50.88 percent of respondents thought that same-sex marriage was extremely or very important, and 79.19 percent of these same respondents considered health care to be extremely or very important.

4. Our sample of students was varied, as 48 (6.15%) of our students are currently or have been in the military. In addition, our sample includes 189 (30.29%) males, and 435 (69.71%) females. Further, our sample includes 525 (84%) whites, 52 African Americans (8.32%), 16 (2.56%) Hispanics, and six (0.96%) Asian Americans. While these attributes could suggest that our sample is predominantly female and white, it is roughly consistent with the population of undergraduate students at this institution, as female undergraduates comprise approximately 53 percent of the population, and whites comprise 75 percent of the student body. Finally, the average age of undergraduates at this institution is 21.1.

5. These were the only questions asked about peer civic experiences in the survey. Some respondents replied that they did not know for one or more of these questions. We coded values for these variables as missing for the purposes of index construction. Thus, no peer civic engagement score exists for those who answered "don't know" for at least one of the questions.

6. It is possible that interest in politics, strong partisanship, and being a political science major are interrelated such that the individual effects of each variable are muted by including all of them in the same model. To consider this possibility, we removed each of these variables, one at a time to investigate whether our results change. When we did so, the results are identical to those that are reported here, with one exception: interest in politics becomes positive and statistically significant when we examine contacting government officials.

7. We acknowledge that there were other issues that surrounded each of these elections. In 2012, though, there were two other issues that were salient: same-sex marriage and health care. When we include opinions about both issues in the models (coded in the same way as the economy), the signs and significance patterns of our results hold with the exceptions that follow. First, taking a political science course was not significant when we examined contacting government officials, but was positive and significant in the remaining models. Second, online political expression and peer civic experiences were not significant when we examine contacting government officials. Third, frequency of

blog reading, peer civic experiences, and interest in politics are no longer significant when we examine participating in protests. Fourth, online political expression is now positive and statistically significant when we examine joining political groups.

In addition, opinions about President Obama's handling of same-sex marriage are not statistically significant predictors in any of the models. However, disapproval of President Obama's handling of health care was positive and statistically significant when we examine joining political groups and contacting newspapers. Otherwise, the health care variables were not statistically significant.

We did not include opinions about President Obama's handling of same-sex marriage or health care for a few statistically based reasons. First, the correlation between opinions about his handling of the economy and health care is 0.786. This is high enough to disturb the remaining model coefficients, given the number of observations in the dataset. Second, those who strongly disapproved of President Obama's handling of the economy were also highly correlated with strongly disapproving of his handling of health care (r = 0.78) and his handling of same-sex marriage (r = 0.50). These correlations are high enough to disturb the values of other model coefficients given the number of survey respondents.

8. A drawback to using this approach is that some ease of interpretation is lost when analyzing the results.

We employed the following formula to calcuilate all of the percentage increase in odds ratios for the ordered logistic regressions:

$$\%\text{OR}_{\text{Increase}} = (e^{\beta} - 1) * 100$$

9. To compute the changes in predicted probabilities, all values for continuous variables were held at their mean and all binary variables at zero. To compute the change for each variable, we changed the value from the mean to one standard deviation above it if it was a continuous variable, and from zero to one for each binary variable, while holding all others at their baseline values.

References

Abel, Jaison R., Richard Dietz, and Yaqin Su. 2014. "Are Recent College Graduates Finding Good Jobs?" *Current Issues in Economics and Finance* 20: 1–8. Available at http://www.newyorkfed.org/research/current_issues/ci20-1.pdf. Accessed on July 15, 2014.

Aristotle 350 BC. *Politics*, Books One through Eight.

Best, Samuel J. and Krueger, Brian S. 2005. "Analyzing the Representativeness of Internet Political Participation." *Political Behavior* 27: 183–216.

Bloom, Joel. 2003. "The Blogosphere: How a Once-Humble Medium Came to Drive Elite Media Discourse and Influence Public Policy and Elections." Paper presented at the annual meeting of the American Political Science Association, Philadelphia, PA.

California State University System. 2014. "American Institutions Requirement." Available at https://secure.csumentor.edu/planning/transfer/inst_requirement.asp. Accessed on July 8, 2014.

Campbell, David E. 2008. "Voice in the Classroom: How an Open Classroom Climate Fosters Political Engagement among Adolescents." *Political Behavior* 30: 437–454.

Campbell, Angus, Phillip Converse, Warren Miller, and Donald Stokes. 1960. *The American Voter*. Chicago, IL: University of Chicago Press.

Center for Information and Research on Civic Learning and Engagement (CIRCLE). 2014. "High School Civics Requirements and Assessments Vary Across the U.S." Available at http://www.civicyouth.org/high-school-civics-requirements-and-assessments-vary-across-the-u-s/?cat_id=10. Accessed on July 3, 2014.

Curtiss, Anthony. 2014. "The Brief History of Social Media." Available at http://www2.uncp.edu/home/acurtis/NewMedia/SocialMedia/SocialMediaHistory.html. Accessed on July 8, 2014.

Dahl, Robert A. 1991. *Democracy and Its Critics*. New Haven, CT: Yale University Press.

Dahl, Robert A. 2006. *A Preface to Democratic Theory*. Chicago, IL: University of Chicago Press.

Dugan, Andrew. 2013. "Democrats Enjoy 2–1 Advantage over GOP among Hispanics. Gallup Politics. Released February 19." Available at http://www.gallup.com/poll/160706/democrats-enjoy-advantage-gop-among-hispanics.aspx. Accessed on July 11, 2014.

Eagan, Kevin, Jennifer B. Lozano, Sylvia Hurtado, and Matthew H. Case. 2013. *The American Freshman: National Norms Fall 2013*. Los Angeles, CA: Higher Education Research Institute, UCLA.

Feldman, Lauren, Josh Pasek, Daniel Romer, and Kathleen Hall Jamieson. 2007. "Identifying Best Practices in Civic Education: Lessons from the Student Voices Program." *American Journal of Education* 114: 75–100.

Flanagan. Constance and Peter Levine 2010. "Civic Engagement and the Transition to Adulthood." *Future Child* 20: 159–179.

Gainous, Jason and Allison M. Martens. 2012. "The Effectiveness of Civic Education: Are "Good" Teachers Actually Good for 'All' Students?" *American Politics Research* 40: 232–266.

Galston, William A. 2001. "Political Knowledge, Political Engagement and Civic Education." *Annual Review of Political Science* 4: 217–234.

Galston, William A. 2004. "Civic Education and Political Participation." *PS: Political Science and Politics* 37: 263–266.

Gibson, Cynthia and Peter Levine 2003. *The Civic Mission of Schools.* New York, NY: Carnegie Corporation of New York and the Center for Information and Research on Civic Learning and Engagement.

Gil de Zuniga, Homero, Eulalia Puig-I-Abril, and Hernando Rojas. 2009. "Weblogs, Traditional Sources Online and Political Participation: An Assessment of How the Internet Is Changing the Political Environment." *New Media & Society* 11: 553–574.

Gimpel, James G., Frances E. Lee, and Joshua Kaminski. 2006. "The Political Geography of Campaign Contributions." *The Journal of Politics* 68: 626–639.

Jefferson, Thomas. 1903. *The Writings of Thomas Jefferson.* Memorial Edition, Vol. 15. Washington DC: Thomas Jefferson Memorial Association.

Kahne, Joseph E. and Joel Westheimer. 2006. "The Limits of Political Efficacy: Educating Citizens for a Democratic Society." *PS: Political Science and Politics* 39: 289–296.

Kahne, Joseph E. and Susan E. Sporte. 2008. "Developing Citizens: The Impact of Civic Learning Opportunities on Students' Commitment to Civic Participation." *American Education Research Journal* 45: 738–766.

Kenski, Kate and Natalie Jomini Stroud. 2006. "Connections between Internet Use and Political Efficacy, Knowledge, and Participation." *Journal of Broadcasting and Electronic Media* 50: 173–192.

King, Gary, Michael Tomz, and Jason Wittenberg. 2000. "Making the Most of Statistical Analyses: Improving Interpretation and Presentation." *American Journal of Political Science* 44: 341–355.

Klofstad, Casey A. 2015. "Exposure to Political Discussion in College Is Associated with Higher Rates of Political Participation Over Time." *Political Behavior* 32: 292–309.

Langton, Kenneth P. and M. Kent Jennings. 1968. "Political Socialization and the High School Civics Curriculum in the United States." *The American Political Science Review* 62: 852–867.

Levine, Peter and Mark Hugo Lopez. 2002. *Youth Voter Turnout has Declined by Any Measure.* Center for Information and Research on Civic Learning and Engagement. Available at http://civicyouth.org/research/products/Measuring_Youth_Voter_Turnout.pdf. Accessed on June 8, 2015.

Lewis, Mitzi. 2011. "An Analysis of the Relationship Between Political Blog Reading, Online Political Activity, and Voting During the 2008 Presidential Campaign." *The International Journal of Interdisciplinary Social Sciences* 6: 11–28.

Lewis-Beck, Michael S. 1990. *Economics and Elections: The Major Western Democracies.* Ann Arbor: University of Michigan Press.

McClurg, Scott D. 2003. "Social Networks and Political Participation: The Role of Social Interaction in Explaining Political Participation." *Political Research Quarterly.* 56: 449–464.

Miller, Warren E. and J. Merrill Shanks. 1996. *The New American Voter.* Cambridge, MA: Harvard University Press.

Min, Seong-Jae 2007. "Online vs. Face-to-Face Deliberation: Effects on Civic Engagement." *Journal of Computer-Mediated Communication* 12(4), article 11. Available at http://jcmc.indiana.edu/vol12/issue4/min.html. Accessed on June 8, 2015.

Moffett, Kenneth W. and Laurie L. Rice. 2014. "College Students and Online Political Expression during the 2008 and 2012 Elections." Working Paper. Southern Illinois University Edwardsville.

Niemi, Richard G. and Jane Junn. 1998. *Civic Education: What Makes Students Learn.* New Haven, CT: Yale University Press.

Norris, Pippa. 1998. "Virtual Democracy." *Harvard International Journal of Press/Politics* 3: 1–4.

Oros, Andrew L. 2007. "Let's Debate: Active Learning Encourages Student Participation and Learning." *Journal of Political Science Education* 3: 293–311.

Pew Research Center for the People and the Press. 2012a. "Assessing the Representativeness of Public Opinion Surveys. Released May 15." Available at http://www.people-press.org/2012/05/15/assessing-the-representativeness-of-public-opinion-surveys. Accessed on September 1, 2013.

Pew Research Center for the People and the Press. 2012b. "In Changing News Landscape, Even Television is Vulnerable." Released September 27. Available at: http://www.people-press.org/files/legacy-pdf/2012%20News%20Consumption%20Report.pdf. Accessed on July 15, 2014.

Rice, Laurie L., Kenneth W. Moffett, and Ramana Madupalli. 2013. "Campaign-Related Social Networking and the Political Participation of College Students." *Social Science Computer Review* 31: 257–279.

Rosenstone, Steven and John Mark Hansen. 1993. *Mobilization, Participation and Democracy in America.* New York: Macmillan.

Rousseau, Jean-Jacques. 1762. *The Social Contract, or Principles of Political Right.*

Shah, Dhavan V., Nojin Kwak, and R. Lance Holbert. 2001. "'Connecting' and 'Disconnecting' with Civic Life: Patterns of Internet Use and the Production of Social Capital." *Political Communication* 18:141–162.

Shah, Dhavan V., Jaeho Cho, William P. Eveland, and Nojin Kwak. 2005. "Information and Expression in a Digital Age: Modeling Internet Effects on Civic Participation." *Communication Research* 32: 531–565.

The University of Texas. 2014. "Government Courses: Legislative Requirement." Available at http://www.utexas.edu/student/admissions/ate/problems/government.html. Accessed on July 8, 2014.

Thies, Cameron G. and Robert E. Hogan. 2005. "The State of Undergraduate Research Methods Training in Political Science." *PS: Political Science and Politics* 38: 755–763.

Thompson, Clive 2006. "The Early Years." *New York*. February 20. Available at http://nymag.com/news/media/15971. Accessed on July 8, 2014.

Tolbert, Caroline J. and Ramona S. McNeal. 2003. "Unraveling the Effects of the Internet on Political Participation?" *Political Research Quarterly* 56: 175–185.

Towner, Terri L. 2013. "All Political Participation Is Socially Networked?: New Media and the 2012 Election." *Social Science Computer Review* 31: 527–541.

Towner, Terri L. and David A. Dulio. 2011. "An Experiment of Campaign Effects during the YouTube Election." *New Media & Society* 13: 626–644.

Verba, Sydney and Norman H. Nie. 1972. *Participation in America: Political Democracy and Social Equality*. New York, NY: Harper and Row.

Verba, Sydney, Kay Lehman Schlozman, and Henry E. Brady. 1995. *Voice and Equality: Civic Voluntarism in American Politics*. Cambridge, MA: Harvard University Press.

Wallsten, Kevin. 2007. "Agenda Setting and the Blogosphere: An Analysis of the Relationship between Mainstream Media and Political Blogs." *Review of Policy Research* 24 (6): 567–587.

Washington, George. 1796. "Farewell Address." Available at http://avalon.law.yale.edu/18th_century/washing.asp. Accessed on July 13, 2014.

Wellman, Barry, Anabel Quan Hasse, James White, and Keith Hampton. 2001. "Does the Internet Increase, Decrease, or Supplement Social Capital?" *American Behavioral Scientist* 45: 436–455.

Zukin, Cliff, Scott Keeter, Molly Andolina, Krista Jenkins, and Michael X. Delli Carpini. 2006. *A New Engagement? Political Participation, Civic Life, and the Changing American Citizen*. New York City: Oxford University Press.

CHAPTER 2

Civic and Political Engagement Outcomes in Online and Face-to-Face Courses

Tanya Buhler Corbin and Allison K. Wisecup

INTRODUCTION

In recent years, two significant trends in higher education have emerged in the scholarship of teaching and learning research (SoTL). In response to the declining levels of civic engagement in America identified by Putnam (2000) and others, scholars, particularly in political science, turned their attention to identifying ways to create pedagogies that cultivate students' civic and political engagement. Through this scholarship, scholars and educators have significantly increased knowledge about the development and implementation of effective pedagogies of engagement. Recent scholarship has shifted from identifying pedagogies of engagement, and has begun to focus on measuring and assessing the effects that these pedagogies have on students' civic and political engagement. At the same time that scholars identified and began to study declining civic and political engagement, online learning in higher education gained popularity. The number of students enrolling in online courses has continued to increase (Means et al. 2009). Currently, 32 percent of all college students take at least one online course during their studies (Allen and Seaman 2013).

Both trends have sparked extensive research, and as a result, scholars know more about how to develop and incorporate pedagogies of engagement and best practices for online teaching and course design. However, these two important trends in higher education have remained largely disparate areas of inquiry. Much of the research about online education focuses almost exclusively on student learning and satisfaction, but does not examine the effect of course delivery method (online vs. face-to-face) on students' political and civic engagement levels. As online learning occupies an increasing share of college students' learning experiences, it is important to examine whether and to what extent courses delivered online can foster civic and political engagement among learners. This research addresses this gap in civic and political engagement knowledge.

In this study, we compare changes in students' political efficacy and political and civic engagement levels in face-to-face courses with changes among students in online courses. Using a quasi-experimental design, with a pre- and posttest survey, we assess changes in students' political and civic engagement in introductory American government courses, and compare these changes between the online and face-to-face classes. Compared to the students enrolled in the face-to-face courses, students in the online courses felt more efficacious, and made greater gains in civic engagement and political engagement. These results suggest that when online courses are designed using best practices identified in the SoTL research, they can function as well or better in fostering civic and political engagement.

In the section that follows, we review the existing literature about civic and political engagement in face-to-face and online courses, examine the debate regarding the efficacy of online learning, and discuss the importance of political efficacy, and political knowledge more broadly for creating civically engaged citizens. We then discuss the design of the course, including the incorporation of best practices for online course delivery, and methods of the current study. After presenting our results, we discuss the potential of online instruction for engendering students' knowledge of current events and foundational political science knowledge and feelings of internal political efficacy.

CIVIC AND POLITICAL ENGAGEMENT

Putnam's *Bowling Alone* (2000) sounded the alarm on a downward trend in civic and political engagement in America. Political science has taken the lead among the disciplines in addressing the worrisome trends of declining participation and knowledge in civil and political activities identified by Putnam. Teaching civic and political engagement is central to the mission of political science (McCartney et al. 2013a). For the last 15 years, the American Political Science Association (APSA) has supported efforts in the discipline to study and improve civic and political engagement among students, including significant research related to civic engagement and service learning in its many incarnations. APSA created a task force on civic engagement and devoted considerable attention to civic and political engagement at national and regional conferences, and at the annual *APSA Teaching and Learning Conference*. These efforts have yielded significant empirical research results that have bolstered our understanding of how to develop, implement, and evaluate pedagogies of civic engagement (Battistoni 2013).

The civic engagement research identifies the best practices in curriculum design to foster civic engagement. The majority of this research has focused on service learning (e.g., Astin and Sax 1998; Birge, Beaird and Torres 2003; Schumer 2001). The service learning literature informs civic engagement research, but differs in an important way. Service learning activities may not necessarily engage students in politically oriented activities, or be intentionally structured to deepen the specific knowledge or skills associated with developing democratic participation or citizenship. Service learning differs from civic engagement. While scholars have used various definitions for civic engagement in the literature, McCartney et al. (2013b) describes civic engagement as a broad term that encompasses a range of activities designed to help students develop knowledge about community problems and solutions, and actively participate in the deliberation and actions to address problems. Political engagement differs from civic participation in that the activities are specifically political, and students engage in the political process, systems, or with political actors to address problems (McCartney et al. 2013b). Both types of engagement require active participation, critical thinking skills, and deliberation to work toward a solution in the community or political system.

Despite gains in civic engagement research, we still have a limited understanding about the most effective ways to promote multiple dimensions of political engagement among college students (Beaumont et al. 2006). Few studies have examined whether and to what extent students' political engagement changes after taking an introductory level political science course (Banta 2007), but existing data suggests that students increase their levels of political knowledge and political engagement after completing introductory level courses in political science (Huerta and Jozwiak 2008; Martin, Tankersley and Ye 2012).

The most extensive empirical research about political engagement comes from the Carnegie *Political Engagement Project* (PEP), which engaged 21 higher education programs in a project to develop and incorporate "pedagogies of engagement," intended to develop students' political engagement skills and foster critical thinking about their democratic republic (Beaumont et al. 2006). Their assessment results showed gains in political engagement on many dimensions, particularly regarding expectations for future political activity (Beaumont et al. 2006). The survey measures used in the Carnegie PEP provide an opportunity to expand this research beyond the project to use in a variety of types of courses and institutions.

ONLINE EDUCATION

Research regarding the efficacy of online education corresponds to the proliferation of online course offerings and the increase in student enrollment in online courses. Most of the research about online education has focused on assessing whether online instruction is effective, and particularly, whether it can be an equal or better alternative to the traditional face-to-face instruction for student learning. The research yields mixed results, but most of the research concludes that students can learn at least as well in online courses as face-to-face courses when the courses are designed using established best practices from the literature (e.g., Botsch and Botsch 2001; Dolan 2008; Dutton, Dutton, and Perry 2001; M. Johnson 2002; S. D. Johnson et al. 2000; Lim 2002; McLaren 2004; Russell 2001; Thirunarayanan and Perez-Prad 2001). In fact, a recent meta-analysis of online course education learning outcomes found that online learning might be *more* effective than traditional instruction (Means et al. 2009).

A seminal publication regarding the efficacy of online learning is Russell's (1999) *The No Significant Differences Phenomenon*. Russell (1999) suggests that when properly integrated and used, technology does not diminish instruction. Student learning is independent of the instructional medium or technologies employed. Subsequent research expands Russell's work, finding that online courses require students to relinquish passive learning models (Summers et al. 2005) and, as a result, must be much more proactive about their education (Logan et al. 2002). Asynchronous courses can facilitate student engagement with the materials, because the absence of an instructor and the adoption of more active learning approaches serves to reinforce knowledge more than the traditional classroom model (Atkinson and Hunt 2008). Online courses allow students to learn at their own pace, review materials as necessary, and offer flexibility not available from face-to-face classes (York 2008). Although recent research supports the idea that online courses can be equally as effective as traditional brick and mortar classes, not all of the existing research touts the benefits of online teaching. Some suggest that the use of online technologies and the creation of online courses will result in the "McDonaldization" of online education (Ritzer 2004). "McDonaldization" occurs when standardized courses are constructed around generic content and mass produced to be taught by nonspecialized faculty, with efficiency being the primary motivator for offering online courses (Ritzer 2004). Consistent with this critique, others argue that online courses, regardless of how well they are designed, cannot replicate the spontaneity of discussions with faculty and peers available in face-to-face classes (Bok 2003; Rovai and Barnum 2003). Although many online courses employ a variety of pedagogical tools and technologies to facilitate discussion among students and faculty, Summers and colleagues (2005) argue that these tools are incomparable to the dynamic and spontaneous discussions characteristic of face-to-face classes.

Despite a growing body of research about the possible benefits and limitations of online teaching and learning, many scholars note the methodological weaknesses of existing studies. The methodological shortcomings of existing research include the use of small and nonrandom samples, failure to account for possible confounding factors such as differential enrollment patterns in online and face-to-face courses, the inability to reproduce findings across studies, the comparison of student outcomes from courses with different instructors and course materials, and the use of inconsistent outcome measures (Bernard et al. 2004; Jahng, Krug, and Zhang 2007; Means et al. 2009; Urtel 2008). Urtel (2008) demonstrates the power of proper design and measurement. Specifically, when larger samples and consistent measures are used, the results indicate that face-to-face students score higher on identical assessments compared to students in online courses.

This study addresses many of the previous limitations by using a quasi-experimental design that compares change in students' feelings of internal political efficacy, civic engagement, and political engagements between online and face-to-face sections of an Introduction to American Government taught by one instructor during several semesters, with no change in course materials or outcome measures. The course instructor previously taught several sections of the face-to-face course and, in the process, refined course materials, pedagogical techniques, and learning outcomes. The course instructor used these refinements to inform the development of the online sections of the course. The instructor deliberately aimed to maintain as much similarity between the online and face-to-face courses as possible during the completion of *Quality Matters* (QM) training. QM is a training program that is faculty-centered, and involves an extensive peer review process to certify the quality of online and blended courses. After completing the semester-long training course, faculty use the QM rubrics to develop online courses that are then peer reviewed by QM certified faculty.

We eliminate many possible sources of variation by keeping the instructor, course design, and course materials as similar as possible. Further, we are able to increase the external validity of the research by using data from multiple sections of the course taught over multiple semesters. Much of the existing research on the efficacy of online courses relies on data from courses taught only once, which limits the generalizability of the findings. This research uses survey data from students, which allows us to control for other possible confounding factors such as differential enrollment patterns and students' personal, familial, and political contexts. We use regression analysis, which allows for more sophisticated statistical analyses than those commonly found in the research on the efficacy of online courses (i.e., ANOVA and *t*-test analyses). Finally, we are unaware of any previous study that compares the effect of course type (online vs face-to-face) on feelings of internal political efficacy, civic engagement, and political engagement.

CIVIC AND POLITICAL ENGAGEMENT IN ONLINE EDUCATION

Despite a prolific literature about civic engagement and online course pedagogy, there is a dearth of research examining the potential for online education to increase civic and political engagement. Some research examines the potential effectiveness of "e-service learning" or experiential learning when taught in an online format (e.g., Dailey-Herbert et al. 2008; Strait and Souer, 2004; Waldner et al. 2012). However, we were able to identify only one study that examines whether and to what extent introductory level political science courses can increase civic and political engagement levels when taught online. In this study, Jackman (2012) evaluates the effectiveness of experiential elements in an online American state and local government course for increasing student political engagement and finds that students increased their political knowledge and engagement levels after completing the course.

Several studies about online learning have addressed questions that are relevant for civic and political engagement even though they do not explicitly focus on pedagogies of engagement. For example, in a comparative study of online and face-to-face courses, Min (2007) found that deliberation occurred in both online and face-to-face courses, and increased participants' issue knowledge, political efficacy, and willingness to participate in politics. Similarly, several studies have examined the role of online discussion posts and found that the course discussions have an important and positive effect on student learning and critical thinking (e.g., Hamann, Pollock, and Wilson 2009; Williams and Lahman 2011). Because discussion and deliberation are such fundamentally important features for democratic participation, these results indicate that online class environments have the potential to develop students' civic and political engagement.

Overall, the literature indicates that we should expect increases in students' levels of political efficacy, as well as in their propensity for civic and political engagement after they have completed an American politics course. Results from the Carnegie PEP found that students made gains in political engagement along many dimensions, particularly regarding expectations for future political activity. In addition, prior research supports the expectation that when online courses are designed using best practices identified in the literature, they are at least as good at fostering civic and political engagement as traditional face-to-face courses. Based on the literature, we expect that the students who complete online American government courses will increase their propensity for civic and political engagement and political efficacy, as will students who complete face-to-face courses. Further, we expect no differences in engagement and efficacy levels between students in the face-to-face and online courses. Given the dearth of research regarding the ability of online course to engender civic and political engagement, we offer the hypotheses below for the present research.

Theory and Hypotheses

The scholarship on teaching and learning is indeterminate regarding the student learning outcomes of online and face-to-face courses. Although some studies find that students perform equally well in both mediums, other evidence suggests gaps between students enrolled in different course types. The present research moves beyond the existing literature to examine how course type influences students' sense of civic engagement. Drawing from the most recent scholarship about civic engagement (e.g., McCartney et al. 2013a), we conceptualize civic engagement to mean that students have a sense of internal political efficacy, indicate a likelihood of future civic engagement and future political engagement. To our knowledge, no research has explicitly examined the effects of course type on civic engagement beyond the e-service learning research, and none examines political engagement in online courses. The mixed evidence from the literature on the scholarship of teaching and learning leads us to proffer three null hypotheses regarding the effects of course type on dimensions of civic and political engagement.

Hypothesis 1: There will be no significant difference between online and face-to-face students' change in feelings of internal political efficacy.

Hypothesis 2: There will be no significant difference between online and face-to-face students' change in the likelihood of future civic engagement.

Hypothesis 3: There will be no significant difference between online and face-to-face students' change in the likelihood of future political engagement.

Design, Methods, and Measures

Course Design

In order to remain as similar as possible, the online and face-to-face courses were developed to be as similar in design and content as possible. The course sections were introduction to American government courses, and were open to all students enrolled at the University. The course is required for students who major or minor in political science, education, social sciences, or criminal justice, and fulfills a general education requirement for many other students. There are typically fewer than five majors in any given section. The course objectives articulated on the syllabus were identical. The online and face-to-face versions of the courses covered the same course content, used the same web text, and were taught by the same instructor at the same institution. The lecture material contained the same information.

Every attempt was made to employ similar pedagogies and assessment measures in both course formats. As such, both the online and face-to-face versions of the course included multiple-choice exams, written assignments, and student discussions. Online discussions involved the use of discussion board posts and responses, which substituted for the in-class activities and discussion in the traditional face-to-face format. When designing online courses, scholars have voiced concerns about the ability to create a sense of community, facilitate deliberative discussions, and develop students' critical thinking skills outside of the traditional classroom. In fact, these skills are fundamental for participation in democracies and communities. Although the research is far from conclusive, several studies find online discussions and critical thinking to be equal or superior to traditional classroom discussions (e.g., Clawson, Deen, and Oxley 2002; Hamann, Pollock, and Wilson 2009; Wilson, Pollock, and Hamann, 2007; Williams and Lahman 2011). To maintain consistency, there were no pedagogical changes made to the two iterations of the online or face-to-face courses.

Data

The data for the study were obtained solely through pretest and posttest web-based surveys. During the first and last weeks of class, students were invited to participate in the study, and participation was voluntary. Students accessed Qualtrics survey links through the electronic course management page dedicated to the class. Students who completed the survey were awarded extra credit equivalent to one quiz grade in the course. If students did not wish to participate, they were offered an equivalent alternate extra credit opportunity, which only one student opted to complete, because the student was not at least 18 years old at the time of the initial data collection. Both surveys required approximately 15–20 minutes to complete and were comprised of measures adapted from the Carnegie PEP survey, and were available for one week at the beginning and end of the semester. A total of 188 students were enrolled in the courses used in the research (55 students in online sections and 133 students in face-to-face sections. The final sample includes 94 complete observations (matched pretest and post-test surveys) for a response rate of 50 percent. Online students contributed 39 observations and face-to-face students contributed 55 observations to the final sample. Respondents provided informed consent online and provided the last four digits of their phone number. Phone number information was used to link student pretest and posttest observations.

Measures[1]

We use three variable sets in the present research, including students' sociodemographic characteristics, aspects of students' political contexts, and whether the students were enrolled in an online or face-to-face section of the course. We employ three relevant sociodemographic indicators: *gender* (male = 1, female = 0), *race* (white = 1, nonwhite = 0), and *class standing*. When exploring possible differences in online and face-to-face classes, we controlled for several confounding factors that could potentially contribute to changes in students' feelings of political efficacy, civic engagement, and political engagement such as students' personal, familial, and academic political contexts. Students indicated the frequency with which they *discussed politics at school* and *discussed politics at home* on a five-point scale ranging from never (0) to very often, more than once a week (4). Students also indicated whether they had ever enrolled in another class with a *requirement* to keep up with politics or the news (1 = yes, 0 = no). We asked students to indicate whether they remember their parents getting a daily *newspaper* when they were growing up (1 = yes, 0 = no or do not know). Students also indicated whether they remember anyone in their home *volunteering* when they were growing up (1 = yes, 0 = no or don't know). Finally, we asked students to indicate their knowledge of *parental voting* while they were growing up.

Knowledge of the frequency of parental voting is measured on a four-point scale ranging from no or don't know (0) to every election (4).

Our dependent variables are change in students' self-reported *internal political efficacy, future civic engagement,* and *future political engagement.* The scales used to derive change scores for each dependent variable are adopted from the Carnegie PEP. Internal political efficacy refers to "beliefs about one's own competence to understand and participate effectively in politics" (Niemi, Craig, and Mattei 1991: 1407.) The internal political efficacy scale is comprised of five items that measure various dimensions of the concept of internal political efficacy. The five items ask students to indicate the extent to which they agree with statements using a five-point Likert scale ranging from very strongly disagree to very strongly agree.[2] The items assess students' feelings about the extent to which they agree or disagree with the following statements: (1) "I feel that I have a pretty good understanding of the political issues facing this country"; (2) "I believe I have a role to play in the political process"; (3) "when political issues are being discussed, I usually have something to say"; (4) "I think I am better informed about politics and government than most people"; and (5) "I consider myself well qualified to participate in the political process." Responses to the individual items are summed and divided by five to produce an average measure of expected internal political efficacy for each student for the pretest and posttest survey administration.

Operational definitions for civic and political engagement vary depending on the study. Although some scholars (e.g., Colby et al. 2003 and Levine 2007) view the two types of engagement as conceptually distinct, others (e.g., Macedo et al. 2005) argue that the types of engagement are too similar to draw a clear line demarcating one from the other. We contend that civic and political engagement are conceptually distinct and borrow the definitions offered by McCartney et al. (2013b). Colby and colleagues (2010) develop two scales that we believe accurately measure and reflect the underlying conceptual hallmarks of civic and political engagement. McCartney notes that civic engagement is a larger more encompassing concept and refers to "...an individual's activities, alone or as part of a group, that focus on developing knowledge about the community and its political system, identifying of seeking solutions to community problems, pursuing goals to benefit the community, and participating in constructive deliberation among community members about the community's political system and community issues, problems, or solutions" (McCartney et al. 2013b: 14). Ultimately, civic engagement involves an attempt to influence the community and includes a wide range of activities, "...such as collecting and disseminating information; voting; working voter registration drives; designing, distributing, or signing petitions; participating in civic and political associations; attending public meetings, rallies, or protests; and entering into public or private discussions of community and political issues via various formats" (McCartney et al. 2013b: 14).

Colby and colleagues (2010) include a scale in the Carnegie PEP that reflects the various behaviors included in the operational definition of civic engagement offered by McCartney et al. (2013b).[3] The civic engagement scale is comprised of seven items that measure students' self-reports of the activities in which they expect to engage in the future. The individual items are measured on a five-point Likert scale ranging from will certainly *not* do this (0) to will certainly *do* this (4). The items assess students' expectations for expressing their political voice in seven distinct activities in the future: (1) "Contact or visit a public official—at any level of government—to ask for assistance or to express your opinion"; (2) "contact a newspaper or magazine to express your opinion on an issue"; (3) "Call in to a radio or television talk show to express your opinion on a political issue"; (4) "Take part in a protest, march, or demonstration"; (5) "Sign a written or e-mail petition about a political or social issue"; (6) "NOT buy something to boycott it because of conditions under which the product is made, or because you dislike the conduct of the company that produces it"; and (7) "Work as a canvasser going door to door for a political candidate or cause." Responses to the individual items are summed and divided by seven to produce an average measure of expected electoral activity for each student for the pretest and posttest survey administration.

McCartney notes that "...political engagement refers to explicitly politically oriented activities that seek a direct impact on political issues, systems, relationships, and structures" (2013b: 14). The activities included in political engagement may have direct or indirect political implications. McCartney suggests "...participating in a community recycling program or working with a local youth group may not necessarily have an explicit political goal, though these may have a community goal and indirect political implications" (2013b: 14). Other activities, however, may have more explicit political goals such as "...working to enact community laws regarding recycling or gain government aid for low-income school districts..." (2013b: 14).

Colby and colleagues (2010) include a scale in the Carnegie PEP that reflects the various behaviors included in the operational definition of political engagement offered by McCartney et al. (2013b).[4] The political engagement scale is comprised of three questions that measure students' self-reports of the political engagement activities in which they expect to participate in the future. The individual items are measured on a five-point Likert scale ranging from will certainly *not* do this (0) to will certainly *do* this (4). The items assess students' expectations for participating in three distinct political engagement activities in the future: (1) "work with a political group or volunteer with a campaign"; (2) "wear a campaign button, put a sticker on your car, or place a sign in front of your house"; (3) "give money to a political candidate or cause." Responses to the individual items are summed and divided by three to produce an average measure of expected electoral activity for each student for the pretest and posttest survey administration.

To produce the change variables, students' scores from the pretest are subtracted from the posttest scores. The change score method for regression analyses is more appropriate than the regressor method for data collected using a nonequivalent control group or quasi-experimental design. Specifically, the latter is more likely to lead to "...the conclusion that there is no treatment effect when a straightforward examination of the means suggests otherwise" (Allison 1990: 99). As such, we employ the change scores as the most appropriate dependent variable for each outcome given the quasi-experimental design of the study.

Analysis

The data are analyzed using ordinary least squares (OLS) regression. Our primary question is whether students enrolled in online and face-to-face courses differ with regard to change in internal political efficacy, future civic engagement, and future political engagement. Although a significant body of research compares a variety of outcomes by type of classroom (e.g., online vs face-to-face), little research directly examines whether classroom type affects the civic engagement variables presently under consideration. As such, we begin with a zero-order model that demonstrates the difference between face-to-face and online students (course type) and then introduce a variety of control variables in subsequent models to estimate if and how the initial relationship between course type and the dependent variables is modified. The second model introduces three demographic control variables: gender, race, and class standing. The third model, the fully saturated model, introduces the personal, familial, and academic political context variables. This iterative process allows us to see how controlling for possible confounding factors may account for the relationship between course type and the dependent variables.

All three hypotheses in the current study are, effectively, null hypotheses. That is, the hypotheses anticipate no significant differences between students in online and face-to-face courses for each of the dependent variables. We employ three OLS regression models to test each of the hypotheses. For each dependent variable, the first model is a zero-order regression model, wherein we regress the dependent variable on course type (online or face-to-face). In the second model, we introduce three sociodemographic variables to determine whether any initial differences in the dependent variable can be attributed to possible differences in enrollment patterns between online and face-to-face courses. Finally, in the third model, we introduce a series of personal, familial, and academic political context variables to determine if any remaining differences in the dependent variable can be attributed to differences in the political contexts of students enrolled in online and face-to-face courses.

Using the above strategy for hypothesis testing can result in drawing inaccurate conclusions because the introduction of variables in models 2 and 3 will, by default, increase the performance of each progressive model. That is, models containing more variables will always explain more of the variation in the dependent variable compared to models with fewer variables. Importantly, because the models are nested, we can estimate whether the introduction of more variables in results in a significant increase in the performance of the model. Two models are nested if one model (full model) contains all the variables in another model (reduced model), plus at least one additional variable. As such, Model 1 is nested in Model 2, Model 1 is nested in Model 3, and Model 2 is nested in Model 3. Comparing the relative performance of nested models is important because the addition of predictors will naturally increase the variance explained, but also increases the likelihood of committing a

Type 1 error with regard to individual coefficients in the model. Rather than testing each coefficient individually, we conduct a global test that estimates whether the coefficient of at least one of the variables in the more complex model is not equal to zero. Calculating an F-statistic using nested models is calculated as:

$$\frac{\dfrac{[\mathrm{SSE_{RM}} - \mathrm{SSE_{FM}}]}{[k]}}{\left[\dfrac{\mathrm{SSE_{FM}}}{n-k+1}\right]} \qquad 2.1$$

where $\mathrm{SSE_{RM}}$ is the sum of squared errors for the reduced model, $\mathrm{SSE_{FM}}$ is the sum of squared errors for the full model, k = number of additional predictors in the full model, and n is the number of observations.

When comparing the models, we begin by reporting the *F*-test statistics for each comparison and then focus our discussion on the preferred model.

RESULTS

Table 2.1 presents the univariate statistics for the variables in the study. The descriptive statistics in Table 2.1 indicate few differences between students of the two types of classes for most of the control variables. Notably, students in online sections of the course tended to be juniors and those in face-to-face sections tended to be sophomores. The only other significant difference between students in the two groups was with regard to knowledge of volunteering in the home. A chi-square test of independence revealed a significant interaction between volunteering in the home and class type [$\chi^2 (1) = 6.799$, $p < 0.01$]. Students in online classes (63%) were more likely to report volunteering in the home compared to students in face-to-face classes (53%). With only two exceptions then, students in the two types of courses are similar for most of the control variables used in the analyses.

Table 2.1 Descriptive statistics for variables in analysis by type of course

	Range	Face-to-face classes (n = 55)		Online classes (n = 39)		Difference in means
		M	SD	M	SD	
Control variables						
Gender (male)	1	0.36	0.49	0.38	0.49	0.02
Race (white)	1	0.80	0.40	0.64	0.49	−0.16
Class standing	4	2.15	0.87	3.30	0.80	1.15***
Talk about politics at home	4	1.93	1.37	2.17	1.38	0.24
Talk about politics in high school	4	2.16	1.17	2.19	1.17	0.03
Daily newspaper	1	0.65	0.48	0.56	0.50	−0.09
Volunteering in household	1	0.35	0.48	0.62	0.49	0.27**
Knowledge of parental voting	3	2.55	0.79	2.70	0.57	0.15
Class requirement	1	0.53	0.50	0.56	0.50	0.03
Dependent variables						
Change in internal political efficacy	5.4	0.35	0.66	0.78	1.11	0.43*
Change in future civic engagement	6.0	0.26	0.99	0.63	1.04	0.37†
Change in future political engagement	7.67	−0.65	1.65	0.38	1.20	1.03**

Note: The Mann–Whitey *U*-test (nonparametric test of differences in mean scores) was used to determine the significance of the difference in means across course types for ordinal and ratio variables. A chi-square test of independence was used to determine whether the occurrence of the variables was independent of class type.
†$p < 0.10$, *$p < 0.05$, **$p < 0.01$, ***$p < 0.001$, using a two-tailed *t*-test.

Table 2.1 also includes the univariate statistics for the dependent variables under investigation. The results indicate significant differences between students in face-to-face and online classes for each of the three variables. An independent samples *t*-test comparing the mean efficacy change scores of students in online and face-to-face classes reveals a significant difference between the means of the two groups [$t (50.925) = 2.128$, $p = 0.02$]. The mean for students enrolled in online sections of the course was significantly higher ($m = 0.78$, $SD = 1.11$) than the mean for students enrolled in face-to-face sections of the course (m = 0.35, SD = 0.66). The univariate results show that students in online sections of the course feel more efficacious at the conclusion of the course compared to students in face-to-face sections. The results in Table 2.1 indicate no significant differences between students enrolled in online and face-to-face sections of the course with regard to civic engagement [t (90) = 1.720, p = 0.09]. The mean for students enrolled in the online sections of the course was higher (m = 0.63, SD = 1.04) than the mean for students enrolled in face-to-face sections of the course (m = 0.26, SD = 0.99), though the difference is not significant. Therefore, students enrolled in online sections of the course are not significantly more likely to be civically engaged at the conclusion of the course compared to students enrolled in face-to-face sections of the course. Finally, the results in Table 2.1 indicate a significant difference between the two groups with regard to future political engagement. An independent samples t-test comparing the mean future political engagement scores of students in online and face-to-face classes reveals a significant difference between the means of the two groups [t (89.441) = 3.457, p = 0.001]. The mean for students enrolled in online sections of the course was significantly higher (m = 0.38, SD = 1.20) than the mean for students enrolled in face-to-face sections of the course (m = −0.65, SD = 1.65). Interestingly, students in online sections of the course not only anticipate greater political engagement at the conclusion of the course; students enrolled in face-to-face sections of the course actually lose ground with regard to expected political engagement. The results in Table 2.1 indicate that there may be differences in the dependent variables associated with course type; however, it remains unclear if these differences persist when controlling for sociodemographic and political context variables.

Table 2.2 contains the OLS regression results pertaining to the first hypothesis that there will be no significant difference between online and face-to-face students' change in feelings of internal political efficacy. A comparison of the models indicates

Table 2.2 Ordinary Least Squares (OLS) regression models predicting change in internal political efficacy

Independent and control variables	Model 1	Model 2	Model 3
Course type (online)	0.438*	0.325	0.404†
	(0.186)	(0.202)	(0.218)
Gender (male)		−0.269	−0.243
		(0.182)	(0.184)
Race (white)		0.083	0.013
		(0.205)	(0.211)
Class standing		0.182†	0.159
		(0.104)	(0.114)
Talked about politics at home			0.162†
			(0.087)
Talked about politics in high school			−0.168†
			(0.094)
Knowledge of parental voting			0.023
			(0.136)
Parents received daily newspaper			−0.032
			(0.199)
Volunteering in the home			−0.257
			(0.205)
Class requiring attention to news			0.178
			(0.177)
Intercept	0.345**	−0.013	0.091
	(0.117)	(0.311)	(0.466)
R^2	0.059	0.130	0.201

†$p < 0.10$, *$p < 0.05$, ** $p < 0.01$, $p < 0.001$, using a two-tailed test. Unstandardized coefficients reported with standard errors in parentheses.

that Model 2 [$F(3, 84) = 5.411$, $p = 0.002$] and Model 3 [$F(9, 77) = 2.591$, $p = 0.01$] are preferred to Model 1. However, a final comparison indicates that Model 2 is preferred to Model 3 [$F(6, 80) = 1.081$, $p = 0.34$]. Thus, of the models in Table 2.2, Model 2 exhibits superior performance. Overall, the model supports the hypothesis of no difference. Although Model 1 indicates a significant, zero-order effect for class type, as was demonstrated in the univariate statistics, the preference for Model 2 suggests that this effect is likely a result of different course enrollment patterns in online and face-toface classes. Recall that the results for the univariate statistics indicate a significant difference in class standing between online and face-

Table 2.3 Ordinary Least Squares (OLS) regression models predicting change in future civic engagement

Independent and control variables	Model 1	Model 2	Model 3
Course type (online)	0.339†	0.322	0.329
	(0.214)	(0.257)	(0.590)
Gender (male)		−0.011	0.009
		(0.227)	(0.235)
Race (white)		0.182	0.207
		(0.253)	(0.267)
Class standing		0.059	0.090
		(0.131)	(0.145)
Talked about politics at home			0.095
			(0.109)
Talked about politics in high school			−0.033
			(0.118)
Knowledge of parental voting			−0.078
			(0.174)
Parents received daily newspaper			−0.202
			(0.254)
Volunteering in the home			−0.090
			(0.258)
Class requiring attention to news			−0.351
			(0.226)
Intercept	0.257†	−0.010	0.329
	(0.136)	(0.382)	(0.590)
R^2	0.032	0.036	0.081

†$p < 0.10$, using a two-tailed test. Unstandardized coefficients reported with standard errors in parentheses.

to-face classes wherein students enrolled in online sections of the course tended to be significantly more advanced than those in face-to-face courses. The nearly significant coefficient associated with the class standing variable in Model 2 suggests that class standing may almost entirely account for initial course type differences in Model 1. More importantly, however, the result for Model 2 indicate that sociodemographic differences almost entirely account for the zero-order effect for class type evident in Model 1. In sum, though Model 2 indicates that students in online classes exhibit greater change in internal political efficacy, the differences between the groups is not significantly different after accounting for students' sociodemographic characteristics.

Furthermore, personal, familial, and academic context variables do not contribute to student gains in feelings of internal political efficacy.

Table 2.3 contains the OLS regression results pertaining to the second hypothesis that there will be no significant difference between online and face-to-face students' change in civic engagement. A comparison of the models in Table 2.3 indicates that Model 1 is superior to Model 2 $[F(3, 85) = 0.39, p = 0.76]$ and Model 3 $[F(9, 78) = 0.56, p = 0.82]$.[5] Model 1 indicates a significant, zero-order effect for class type, as was demonstrated in the univariate statistics. That is, students enrolled in online courses demonstrate significantly greater gains in civic engagement compared to students enrolled in face-to-face courses. Specifically, students in online sections report a greater propensity for civic engagement at the conclusion of the course compared to students enrolled in face-to-face sections of the course. Further, the differences between students in online and face-to-face sections does not result from differential patterns of enrollment (Model 2) or personal, familial, or educational political contexts (Model 3). Ultimately, then, the results in Table 2.3 fail to support the Hypothesis 2 of no difference between online and face-to-face students with regard to change in civic engagement.

Table 2.4 presents the OLS regression results for the third hypothesis, which posits that there will be no significant difference in change in political engagement associated with course type. A comparison of the nested models in Table 2.4 indicates that Model 1 is preferred to Model 2 $[F(3, 84) = 0.70, p = 0.56]$ and Model 3 $[F(9, 77) = 0.95, p = 0.49]$.[6] Model 1 indicates a significant, zero-order effect for class type, as was demonstrated in the univariate statistics. That is, students enrolled in online courses demonstrate significantly greater gains in political engagement compared to students enrolled in face-to-face courses. Furthermore, the significant association

Table 2.4 Ordinary Least Squares (OLS) regression models predicting change in future political engagement

Independent and control variables	Model 1	Model 2	Model 3
Course type (online)	1.027**	1.010 **	1.058*
	(0.316)	(0.377)	(0.405)
Gender (male)		0.360	0.378
		(0.334)	(0.339)
Race (white)		−0.093	−0.037
		(0.371)	(0.385)
Class standing		−0.036	0.032
		(0.193)	(0.210)
Talked about politics at home			0.168
			(0.157)
Talked about politics in high school			−0.027
			(0.170)
Knowledge of parental voting			−0.231
			(0.252)
Parents received daily newspaper			−0.539
			(0.366)
Volunteering in the home			0.005
			(0.373)
Class requiring attention to news			−0.571
			(0.327)
Intercept	−0.649	−0.628	0.122
	(0.200)	(0.560)	(0.852)
R^2	0.105	0.108	0.175

$\dagger p < 0.10$, $*p < 0.05$, $**p < 0.01$, $p < 0.001$, using a two-tailed test. Unstandardized coefficients reported with standard errors in parentheses.

between class type and change in political engagement is not explained by differential enrollment patterns (Model 2) or students' political contexts (Model 3). The preferred model (Model 1) indicates that the significant gains associated with course type persist and strengthen with the introduction of sociodemographic variables. The results for Model 1 fail to support the hypothesis of no difference in changes in political engagement and course type.

In sum, the results of the analyses provide mixed support for the study hypotheses. The hypothesis of no difference between course type and internal political efficacy is supported. Although students in online classes exhibited greater gains in feelings of internal political efficacy, the results provide some evidence that enrollment differences in online and face-to-face classes may entirely account for these differences. Similarly, the results support the hypothesis of no significant differences by course type for civic engagement. Students in online and face-to-face sections exhibit similar levels of civic engagement at the conclusion of the course. However, the results fail to support the hypothesis of no significant differences based on course type for changes in political engagement. Specifically, we find that an interesting pattern of outcomes by course type. First, students enrolled in online sections of the course exhibited significantly higher levels of political engagement at the conclusion of the course compared to those enrolled in face-to-face sections. Perhaps more compelling is the finding that the manner in which the differences by course type emerge. Specifically, the results indicate that the differences in political engagement by course type are not simply produced by online students demonstrating greater gains in political engagement, but the gains by students in online courses are accompanied by losses among students enrolled in face-to-face classes. As such, part of the difference in political engagement between students derives from declines in political engagement among those enrolled in face-to-face classes. We address the possible reasons for the mixed results in the discussion and conclusion section.

DISCUSSION AND CONCLUSIONS

This study examines the extent to which students' feelings of internal political efficacy, civic engagement, and political engagement are influenced by course delivery type (online vs face-to-face) in introduction to American government courses. The most frequent, and in some respects, the most important course taught in political science is the Introduction to American government course. This course is required in many states to earn a Bachelor's degree (e.g., California and Texas, among others), and in many other cases, the course fulfills a fundamental core curriculum requirement. In addition, it is also likely to be a student's first, if not final experience with political science concepts. This course provides an introduction to political science and thus may be the vehicle by which students get excited about the discipline, and decide to major or minor in political science. More often, however, this course is the last opportunity the student will have to learn about political science concepts. As such, the introduction to American government course provides an opportunity to develop students' knowledge about citizenship, civic, and political engagement, particularly for students for whom this may be the last and only time they consider this subject. Because this course presents the last opportunity for students who are not political science majors to learn to think critically about their role as citizens, as community members, and as participants in their government, it is a course where incorporating strategies that foster this type of learning are most important.

Similar to Driscoll and colleagues (2012), we improve on previous research regarding the effects of course type in several important ways. First, we employ a quasi-experimental design. The data for the study come from sections of a single course, taught by the same instructor over several terms. As such, we are able to hold constant many possible confounding factors such as course content, subject materials, and the population from which students were drawn. Further, we move beyond the existing literature by examining other relevant student outcomes. Finally, the use of longitudinal data allow us to model change in the dependent variables, rather than simply a comparison of pretest and posttest measures.

Although an increasing body of literature demonstrates there are no significant differences in student learning outcomes between online and face-to-face classes (e.g., Russell 1999; Tucker 2001), other evidence indicates better outcomes for students enrolled in face-to-face classes (Urtel 2008). We depart from conventional measures frequently employed when comparing online and face-to-face classes such as learning, student satisfaction, and course evaluations by exploring whether online classes affect students' feelings of internal political efficacy, civic engagement, and political engagement. A review of the literature suggests that we are the first to explore these specific outcomes through a comparison of online and face-to-face classes. As such, we rely on the broader findings in the scholarship of teaching and learning to contextualize and better understand our mixed findings.

The results of the study partially support a growing body of literature and the study hypotheses, which suggest no systematic differences in outcomes for students, enrolled in online and face-to-face classes. Although we initially find a significant difference in students' feelings of internal political efficacy between students enrolled in different course types, more extensive analyses reveal that the difference is primarily an artifact of differential enrollment patterns, and is not the result of students' personal, familial, or educational contexts. Specifically, having greater numbers of students with advanced class standing enrolled in online classes entirely accounts for the differences in internal political efficacy at the conclusion of the course.

In terms of changes in civic and political engagement, we find mixed results for the expectation of no differences by course type hypothesis. Specifically, students' increases in civic engagement levels do not differ significantly by course type. Although students in online courses demonstrate slightly greater gains than those enrolled in face-to-face courses, the changes are not significant. We find that differential enrollment patterns and students' political context do not explain the differences between the two groups at the end of the course. The results for civic engagement support our expectations and a growing body of literature that suggests online mediums can be efficient conduits for learning. Further, these results provide us with cautious optimism that students will develop greater levels of civic engagement, regardless of whether they enroll in online or face-to-face classes.

An interesting and unexpected finding in the study is the difference in students' political engagement at the conclusion of the course. Not only do students in online courses exhibit significantly greater gains in political engagement at the conclusion of the course, students' political engagement actually declines for those enrolled in face-to-face sections. Furthermore, neither the gains nor losses for either group are explained by differential enrollment patterns or students' personal, familial, or educational political contexts. While more research is needed to understand these unexpected findings, one explanation is important to consider. One difference in the traditional classroom compared to the online course was that during discussions the instructor was able to encourage students to think through the obstacles and challenges to political participation in the American political system. During the course, students increased their understanding of the complexities and nuances of political participation, thus moving away from their initial default position of the K-12 civics version of political engagement. It is plausible that the absence of an instructor "in the room" in online courses meant that students had less exposure to the nuances of the American political system. If this is the case, then the findings that students show higher political engagement levels are misleading, because rather than the online course providing a learning experience that facilitated political engagement, the students missed an important lesson about the political system. This is an important area for future research.

In some respects, it is not surprising to find that students in both course types make gains in civic engagement measures. The measures are broader and more encompassing than those for political engagement are, and the finding that online and face-to-face students both made gains in civic engagement levels after completing the course is consistent with the literature about Millennials. Nearly one-third of all high school students participate in volunteer work, and thus many students come to college with previous experience with or exposure to civic participation (CIRCLE n.d.). Millennials are also more likely to opt for civic participation and nonpolitical engagement than participate in political activities, which they regard with more suspicion (CIRCLE 2010).

The present investigation corrects for many of methodological shortcomings of existing research on the scholarship of teaching and learning in online classes using longitudinal data from students using a quasi-experimental design. The study is quasi-experimental in the sense that students self-selected into online or face-to-face sections of the course. Importantly, Driscoll and colleagues (2012) find differences in online and face-to-face students that go beyond the characteristics explored here. Specifically, the authors find that online students tended to be older, have lower grade point averages (GPA), were more experienced with online classes, were more likely to be seniors, were taking fewer credit hours, and worked more hours per week compared to students enrolled in face-to-face classes. The authors found that these factors were important predictors of student performance and satisfaction. More importantly, they found that GPA was the single best predictor of performance and satisfaction. It is unclear whether these factors would be equally important for understanding political efficacy and civic and political engagement, but future research should explore the extent of differential enrollment patterns and the impact of online learners' academic characteristics more closely. In addition, future studies should replicate this research with different student populations. Our student sample comes from a medium-sized public university in Southwest Virginia, and includes a significant proportion of first-generation and academically underprepared students. While this student demographic is the fastest growing in America, making it an important student population to understand, there are any number of reasons to suspect that our findings may not be generalizable to other college student populations. Many note the rapid growth of online learning (Means et al. 2009) and others note that nearly 30 percent of students enrolled in higher education will enroll in at least one online course during their time in college and that online enrollment is increasing at a faster rate than that of higher education more broadly (Allen and Seaman 2010). Further, Allen and Seaman (2013) note that the proportion of students taking at least one course online has risen to 32 percent. The proliferation of online teaching and learning buttresses our call for more research at the confluence of online learning and civic and political engagement.

We are cautiously optimistic with regard to our findings.—if civic engagement is an important outcome, and we think it is-then online and face-to-face students do not exhibit significant differences in levels of civic engagement. Since this is the first study of this kind, these results provide preliminary evidence, and there is a need for more research in this area. Although the rate of online enrollment has slowed slightly, it continues to outpace enrollment rates of overall higher education (Allen and Seaman 2013). Given these trends, it is clear that online learning will persist as a substantial component of the edifice of higher education. As such, political science scholars and edu-cators must better understand whether student outcomes in introductory political science courses, beyond satisfaction and learning, are comparable among students enrolled in online and face-to-face classes.

Appendix 2.1

Relevant Sections of the Adapted Carnegie Foundation Political Engagement Project: Civic and Political Engagement Outcomes in Online and Face-to-face Courses. (To obtain a copy of the full survey, please contact the corresponding author.)

SECTION B: YOUR PERSPECTIVES ON POLITICAL ACTION (INTERNAL POLITICAL EFFICACY SCALE)

Instructions: Please use the following scale to respond to the statements below.

Table 2.5 Internal political efficacy indicators

	A Very strongly disagree	B Disagree	C Neither agree or disagree	D Agree	E Very strongly agree
B4.1 I feel that I have a pretty good understanding of the political issues facing our country					
B4.2 I believe I have a role to play in the political process					
B4.3 When policy issues or problems are being discussed, I usually have something to say					
B4.4 I think that I am better informed about politics and government than most people					
B4.5 I consider myself well qualified to participate in the political process.					

Section D: Your Expectations about Future Involvement (Political Engagement [PE] and Civic Engagement [CE])

Instructions: Below is a list of things that some people do to express their views or take social or political action. *In the future, what do you expect that you will do?*

Table 2.6 Measures of students' civic and political engagement

	A *Will certainly* **not** *do this*	B	C	D	E *Will certainly* **do** *this*
D1.5 Contact or visit a public official—at any level of government—to ask for assistance or to express your opinion [CE]					
D1.6 Contact a newspaper or magazine to express your opinion on an issue [CE]					
D1.7 Call in to a radio or television talk show to express your opinion on a political issue [CE]					
D1.9 Take part in a protest, march, or demonstration [CE]					
D1.10 Sign a written or e-mail petition about a political or social issue [CE]					
D1.11 Work with a political group or volunteer for a campaign [PE]					
D1.12 NOT buy something or boycott it because of conditions under which the product is made, or because you dislike the conduct of the company that produces it [CE]					
D1.14 Wear a campaign button, put a sticker on your car, or place a sign in front of your house [PE]					
D1.15 Give money to a political candidate or cause [PE]					
D1.16 Work as a canvasser going door to door for a political candidate or cause [CE]					

SECTION E: BACKGROUND INFORMATION

Table 2.7   Measures of students' political contexts

	A Never	B	C	D	E Very often—once a week or more
E1 In your home while you were growing up, how often were political topics discussed?					
E2 In your high school, how often were political topics discussed?					

E3. Did your parents get a daily newspaper at home when you were growing up?

Yes	No

E4. From what you remember growing up, did anyone in your household spend time volunteering?

Yes	No

E5. From what you remember growing up, how often did your parents vote in elections?

Not at all	Rarely	Most elections	Every election	Don't know

E6. Have any of your other college or graduate classes ever required you to keep up with politics or government, either by reading the newspaper, watching TV, or going on the Internet?

Table 2.8 Sociodemographic measures

	Yes	*No*

E7. 37) What is your current student classification in college or graduate school?

Freshman/First-year undergraduate

Sophomore

Junior

Senior

Graduate student (please specify degree and year, such as 1st yr MA)

Unclassified

E8. Your sex

Male

Female

E9. How do you identify yourself racially or ethnically? (Please mark all that apply.)

American Indian or Native American

Asian American or Pacific Islander

Black or African American

Hispanic, Latino, or Spanish origin

White/Caucasian

Other/Additional (please specify)

NOTES

1. The measures described here are in Appendix 2.1.
2. The *Carnegie Political Engagement Project* employs a six-point Likert scale to measure each item in all three scales. Early data collection in a group-administered format using scantron forms prohibited using a six-point scale. To be consistent with our own previous efforts, we retained the five-point scale when data collection transitioned to an Internet survey. Our analyses of the data, available upon request, indicate that the predictive validity of measures is not compromised.

3. The authors refer to the scale as the Future Political Voice scale. We use this scale because it captures the activities expressed in the operational definition offered by McCartney et al. (2013a).
4. The authors refer to the scale as the Future Electoral Action scale. However, we feel that the scale accurately captures the activities expressed in the operational definition offered by McCartney et al. (2013a).
5. The comparisons indicate that Model 2 is preferred to Model 3 [F (6, 81) = 0.15, p = 0.99], but Model 1 outperforms Model 2. Thus, Model 1 is the preferred model.
6. Again, the comparisons indicate that Model 2 is preferred to Model 3 [F (6, 81) = 0.95, p = 0.47), however because Model 1 exhibits superior performance relative to Model 2, we conclude that Model 1 is, overall, the preferred model.

References

Allen, I. Elaine and Jeff Seaman. 2010. *Class Differences: Online Education in the United States.* The Sloan Consortium. Available at http://sloanconsortium.org/publications/survey/class_differences/. Accessed on November 17, 2014.

Allen, I. Elaine and Jeff Seaman. 2013. *Changing Course: Ten Years of Tracking Online Education in the United States.* Sloan Consortium; Babson Survey Research Group; Pearson. Available at http://onlinelearningconsortium.org/survey_report/2013-survey-online-learning-report/. Accessed on November 17, 2014.

Allison, Paul. 1990. "Change Scores as Dependent Variables in Regression Analysis." *Sociological Methodology* 20: 93–114.

Astin, Alexander W. and Linda J. Sax. 1998. "How Undergraduates Are Affected by Service Participation." *Journal of College Student Development* 39 (3): 251–263.

Atkinson, Maxine P. and Andrea N. Hunt. 2008. "Inquiry-Guided Learning in Sociology." *Teaching Sociology* 36 (1): 1–7.

Banta, Trudy. 2007. *Assessing Student Learning in the Disciplines: Assessment Update Collections.* New York: Wiley.

Battistoni, Richard. 2013. "Preface." In *Teaching Civic Engagement: From Student to Active Citizen*, edited by McCartney, Alison Rios Millett, Elizabeth A. Bennion, and Dick Simpson. Washington DC: American Political Science Association.

Beaumont, Elizabeth, Anne Colby, Thomas Ehrlich, and Judith Torney-Purta. 2006. "Promoting Political Competence and Engagement in

College Students: An Empirical Study." *Journal of Political Science Education* 2: 249–270.

Bernard, Robert M., Phillip C. Abrami, Yiping Lou, Evgueni Borokhovski, Anne Wade, Lori Wozney, Peter Andrew Wallet, Manon Fiset, and Binru Huang. 2004. "How Does Distance Education Compare to Classroom Instruction? A Meta-analysis of Empirical Literature." *Review of Educational Research* 74(3): 379–439.

Birge, James, Brooke Beaird, and Jan Torres. 2003. "Partnerships among Colleges and Universities for Service Learning." In *Building Partnerships for Service-Learning*, edited by B. Jacoby. San Francisco: Jossey Bass.

Botsch, Carol S. and Robert E. Botsch. 2001. "Audiences and Outcomes in Online and Traditional American Government Classes: A Comparative Two-Year Case Study." *PS* 34 (2): 135–141.

Bok, Derek. 2003. *Universities in the Marketplace: The Commercialization of Higher Education*. Princeton, NJ: Princeton University Press.

CIRCLE. n.d. "Volunteering Trends and Statistics." Available at http://www.civicyouth.org/quick-facts/volunteeringcommunity-service/#2. Accessed December 12, 2014.

CIRCLE. 2010. "Millennials Talk Politics: A Study of College Student Civic Engagement." Available at http://www.civicyouth.org/PopUps/CSTP.pdf., date accessed December14, 2014.

Clawson, Rosalee A., Rebecca E. Deen, and Zoe M. Oxley. 2002. "Online Discussions across Three Universities: Student Participation and Pedagogy." *PS* 35 (4): 713–718.

Colby, Anne, Elizabeth Beaumont, Thomas Ehrlich, and Josh Corngold. 2007. *Educating for Democracy: Preparing Undergraduates for Political Engagement*. San Francisco: Jossey-Bass.

Dailey-Herbert, Amber, Emily Donnelli-Sallee, and Laurie N. Dipadova-Stocks, eds. 2008. *Service-Elearning: Educating for Citizenship*. Charlotte, NC: Information Age Publishing.

Dolan, Kathleen. 2008. "Comparing Modes of Instruction: The Relative Efficacy of On-Line and In-Person Teaching for Student Learning." *PS* 41(2): 387–391.

Driscoll, Adam, Karl Jicha, Andrea N. Hunt, Lisa Tichavsky, and Gretchen Thompson. 2012. "Can Online Courses Deliver In-Class Results?: A Comparison of Student Performance and Satisfaction in an Online versus a Face-to-Face Introductory Sociology Course." *Teaching Sociology* 40 (4): 312–331.

Dutton, John, Marilyn Dutton, and Joe Perry, 2001. "Do Online Students Perform as Well as Lecture Students?" *Journal of Engineering Education* 90 (1): 131–136.

Hamann, Kerstin, Philip H. Pollock, and Bruce M. Wilson. 2009. "Learning From 'Listening' to Peers in Online Political Science Classes." *Journal of Political Science Education* 5 (1): 1–11.

Huerta, Juan and David Jozwiak. 2008. "Developing Civic Engagement in General Education Political Science." *Journal of Political Science Education* 4 (1): 42–60.

Jackman, Jennifer. 2012. "When Virtuality and Reality Meet: Online Courses, Experiential Learning and Political Engagement." American Political Science Association Teaching and Learning Conference, February 17–19, 2012.

Jahng, Namsook, Don Krug, and Zuochen Zhang. 2007. "Student Achievement in Online Distance Education Compared to Face-to-Face Education." *European Journal of Open, Distance, and E-Learning* 1. Available at http://eurodl.org/materials/contrib/2007/Jahng_Krug_Zhang.htm/. Accessed November 17, 2014.

Johnson, Margaret. 2002. "Introductory Biology Online: Assessing Outcomes of Two Student Populations." *Journal of College Science Teaching* 31 (5): 312–317.

Johnson, Scott D., Steven R. Aragon, Najmuddin Shaik, and Nilda Palma-Rivas. 2000. "Comparative Analysis of Learner Satisfaction and Learning Outcomes in Online and Face-to-Face Learning Environments." *Journal of Interactive Learning Research* 11 (1): 29–49.

Levine, Peter. 2007. *The Future of Democracy: Developing the Next Generation of American Citizens.* Boston: Tufts University Press.

Lim, Doo H. 2002. "Perceived Differences between Classroom and Distance Education: Seeking Instructional Strategies for Learning Applications." *International Journal of Educational Technology* 3 (1). Available at http://www.ed.uiuc.edu/ijet/v3n1/d-lim/index.html. Accessed January 11, 2011.

Logan, Elisabeth, Rebecca Augustyniak, and Alison Rees. 2002. "Distance Education as Different Education: A Student-centered Investigation of Distance Learning Experience." *Journal of Education for Library and Information Science* 43 (1): 32–42.

Macedo, Stephen, Yvette Alex-Assensoh, Jeffrey M. Berry, Michael Brintnall, David E. Campbell, Luis Ricardo Fraga, Archon Fung, William A. Galston, Christopher F. Karpowitz, Margaret Levi, Meira Levinson, Keena Lipsitz, Richard G. Niemi, Robert D. Putnam, Wendy M. Rahn, Rob Reich, Robert R. Rodgers, Todd Swanstrom, and Katherine Cramer Walsh. 2005. *Democracy at Risk: How Political Choices Undermine Citizen Participation and What We Can Do about It.* Washington, DC: Brookings Institution Press.

Martin, Pamela, Holley Tankersley, and Min Ye. 2012. "Are They Living What They Learn?: Assessing Knowledge and Attitude Change in Introductory Politics Courses." *Journal of Political Science Education* 8: 201–223.

McCartney, Alison Rios Millett, Elizabeth A. Bennion, and Dick Simpson, eds. 2013a. *Teaching Civic Engagement: From Student to Active Citizen.* Washington, DC: American Political Science Association.

McCartney, Alison Rios Millett, Elizabeth A. Bennion, and Dick Simpson, eds. 2013b. "Teaching Civic Engagement: Debates, Definitions, Benefits, and Challenges." In *Teaching Civic Engagement: From Student to Active Citizen.* Washington DC: American Political Science Association.

McLaren, Constance H. 2004. "A Comparison of Student Persistence and Performance in Online and Classroom Business Statistics Experiences." *The Decision Sciences Journal of Innovative Education* 2 (1): 1–10.

Means, Barbara, Yukie Toyama, Robert Murphy, Marianne Bakia, and Karla Jones. 2009. "Evaluation of Evidence-Based Practices in Online Learning: A Meta-Analysis and Review of Online Learning Studies." US Department of Education, Office of Planning, Evaluation and Policy Development. Available at http://www2.ed.gov/rschstat/eval/tech/evidence-based-practices/finalreport.pdf. Accessed January 11, 2011.

Min, Seong-Jae. 2007. "Online vs. Face-to-Face Deliberation: Effects on Civic Engagement." *Journal of Computer-Mediated Communication* 12 (4): 1369–1387

Niemi, Richard G., Stephen Craig, and Franco Mattei. 1991. "Measuring Internal Political Efficacy in the 1988 National Election Study." *The American Political Science Review* 85 (4): 1407–1413.

Putnam, Robert. 2000. *Bowling Alone: The Collapse and Renewal of American Community.* New York: Simon & Schuster.

Ritzer, George. 2004. *The McDonaldization of Society,* 4th ed. Thousand Oaks, CA: Pine Forge Press.

Rovai, Alfred P. and Kirk T. Barnum. 2003. "On-line Course Effectiveness: An Analysis of Student Interactions and Perceptions of Learning." *Journal of Distance Education* 18 (1): 57–73.

Russell, Thomas L. 1999. *The No Significant Difference Phenomenon.* Chapel Hill, NC. Office of Instructional Telecommunications: University of North Carolina.

Russell, Thomas L. 2001. *The No Significant Difference Phenomenon: A Comparative Research Annotated Bibliography on Technology for Distance Education*, Montgomery, AL: International Distance Education Certification Center.

Schumer, Robert. 2001. "Service Learning Is for Everybody." In *Developing and Implementing Service Learning Programs*, edited by M. Canada, B. W. Speck, and M. Kramer. San Francisco: Jossey Bass.

Strait, Jean and Tim Sauer. 2004. "Constructing Experiential Learning for Online Courses: The Birth of E-Service." *EDUCAUSE Quarterly* 27 (1): 62–65.

Summers, Jessica J., Alexander Waigandt, and Tiffany A. Whittaker. 2005. "A Comparison of Student Achievement and Satisfaction in an Online Versus Traditional Face-to-Face Statistics Class." *Innovative Higher Education* 56 (4): 233–250.

Thirunarayanan, M. O. and Aiza Perez-Prado. 2001. "Comparing Web-Based and Classroom-Based Learning: A Quantitative Study." *Journal of Research on Computing in Education* 34 (2): 131–137.

Tucker, Shelia. 2001. "Distance Education: Better, Worse, Or as Good as Traditional Education?" *Online Journal of Distance Learning Administration* 4 (4). http://www.westga.edu/~distance/ojdla/winter44/tucker44.html. Accessed November 9, 2014.

Urtel, Mark G. 2008. "Assessing Academic Performance Between Traditional and Distance Education Course Formats." *Educational Technology & Society* 11 (1): 322–330.

Waldner, Leora S., Sue Y. McGorry, and Murray C. Widener. 2012. "E-Service-Learning: The Evolution of Service-Learning to Engage a Growing Online Student Population." *Journal of Higher Education Outreach and Engagement* 16 (2): 123–150.

Williams, Leonard and Mary Lahman. 2011. "Online Discussion, Student Engagement, and Critical Thinking.", *Journal of Political Science Education* 7 (2): 143–162.

Wilson, Bruce M., Philip H. Pollock, and Kerstin Hamann. 2007. "Does Active Learning Enhance Learner Outcomes? Evidence from Discussion Participation in Online Classes." *Journal of Political Science Education* 3 (2): 131–142.

York, Reginald O. 2008. "Comparing Three Modes of Instruction in a Graduate Social Work Program." *Educational Technology & Society* 11 (1): 322–330.

CHAPTER 3

Rethinking the Way We Communicate about Politics with Millennials

Hillary C. Shulman

Although it is rarely framed in this manner, it may be beneficial to think about Millennial disengagement (those born between 1980 and 2000, Zukin et al. 2006) as a communication problem that needs addressing. In other words, rather than take the perspective that Millennials are a politically deficient generation or that political apathy is a pervasive and unavoidable social problem in America's youth, it needs to be considered that media, elites, and educators have not best figured out how to effectively communicate about politics with younger audiences. This is the central conceit of this chapter. Communication scholars are interested in how message features impact audiences in a variety of ways. Although this book prescribes several different approaches for dealing with this issue, the purpose of this chapter is to address this concern from a communication perspective, with the hopes of understanding how communication interventions can be utilized to increase Millennials' civic perceptions.

In order to address the problem of youth civic disengagement it is important to consider theoretically the root causes of this problem. According to Delli Carpini (2000), Millennial disengagement can be attributed to a deficiency in the following domains: motivation, ability, and opportunity. *Motivation* refers to the innate sense of responsibility to participate in political affairs, and the belief that one's behavior or involvement can make a difference. *Abilities* include time, money, information, and communication skills. Finally, *opportunity* refers to the presence of civic infrastructure that supports or encourages political participation, such as political associations, charitable organizations, or religious institutions. Delli Carpini (2000) goes on to argue that without these factors in place, civic engagement is highly unlikely.

Although Delli Carpini (2000) among others (Craig and Maggiotto 1982; Delli Carpini and Keeter 1997; Pinkleton and Austin 2004; Rahn 1998; Zukin et al. 2006) have painted a bleak picture for the political involvement of the Millennial generation, inherent in Delli Carpini's explanations for Millennial disengagement are recommendations for how to address this troubling issue. In order to address Millennial disengagement from a communication perspective, political messaging must seek to instill motivation, improve abilities (or at least perceptions of abilities), and provide opportunities for this generation. As such, this chapter is organized into three sections. Each section begins with an overview of each component from Delli Carpini's (2000) model. Following this overview, each section will highlight some theoretical and empirical examples of emergent work in this domain. It is hoped that the ideas discussed throughout the chapter inspire others who are interested in how to communicate about politics in more strategic and effective ways, regardless of audience.

TARGETING MILLENNIALS' POLITICAL MOTIVATION

Overview

According to Delli Carpini's (2000) model, the *motivation* component of engagement "...derives from a number of sources: a sense that it is your responsibility to do so; the satisfaction that comes from participating with others for a common purpose; the identification of a public problem that affects you or those you care about; and the belief that your involvement will make a difference." (343). Inherent in this definition are two dimensions of motivation. The first refers to a sense of civic duty. The second regards perceptions of political efficacy. As such, this section considers each of these dimensions separately.

Civic Norms

A sense of civic duty arises from social norms that prescribe desirable or acceptable behaviors within a given culture. To quote a seminal text in this regard, Almond and Verba (1963) refer to citizenship norms as "a shared set of expectations about the citizen's role in politics." Although the specifics of these expectations vary somewhat from person to person, Dalton's (2008) research on contemporary citizenship norms finds that Americans overwhelmingly tend to report two types of citizenship norms. The first type refers to *Citizen Duty*, which includes behaviors such as reporting a crime to the police, obeying the law, voting, serving in the military, and participating in jury duty. These norms primarily refer to "norms of social order" and include behaviors that are thought to be essential within a functioning democracy. The second dimension from Dalton's data (2008) was *Engaged Citizen* norms, which represent communitarian norms and autonomy norms. Examples of these behaviors include being active in politics, joining voluntary groups, and forming one's own opinion. Relating these ideas back to Millennial disengagement, a couple of interesting trends become relevant. The first is that Dalton uncovered a positive relationship ($r = 0.20$) between age and duty-based citizenship, revealing that younger Americans are not particularly compelled to act through sense of civic duty or obligation. This finding echoes earlier research from the National Association of Secretaries of State (1998), which found that only 28 percent of 15–24-year-olds mention civic duty as a motivator of voting (compared to a rate of over 50% for those older than 50 years old). Despite this discouraging finding, surprisingly, Dalton's research obtained a negative correlation ($r = -0.05$) between age and engagement-based citizenship, which suggests that younger Americans place a higher value on more active and personalized forms of political participation than older generations. This relationship was more directly corroborated by Basehart and Nagler (2009) who assert:

> Compared to the previous three generations, Millennials are the absolute lowest when it comes to following the news, lower on registering to vote and on always voting. On the other hand Millennials are "holding their own" in the community by volunteering, problem solving and fundraising. For example, Millennials are as active as other generations when it comes to participating in walking, running, or bicycling for a charitable cause. (10)

Applying these trends to communication research in practice, a few practical implications become apparent. First, this research suggests that traditional appeals to motivate political participation, such as appeals that reference traditional American values, may not be particularly effective with a Millennial audience. Moreover, appeals that induce guilt for not participating should also be ineffectual when attempting to target this group. Instead of employing tactics that address Millennials as a part of the broader American citizenry, Dalton's (2008) work implies that Millennials need to be targeted as their own community and need to be motivated by a personal and inspiring cause. Message personalization might resonate particularly well within this demographic given that Millennials report valuing autonomy in their political decision-making, and are more willing to express their political opinions in active ways and through less traditional channels (Delli Carpini 2000). Thus, in order to target this group effectively, and from a normative perspective, communication would be well served to attempt to increase perceptions of political norms through channels and messaging that is more immediate and relevant.

In the communication and social psychology literature, an abundance of work has looked at the relationship between perceptions of social norms and a diverse array of behaviors. This line of research has linked normative perceptions to smoking behavior (e.g., Rhodes et al. 2008), binge drinking (e.g., Rimal and Real 2003, 2005), littering (e.g., Cialdini, Reno, and Kallgren 1990), organ donation (e.g., Park and Smith 2007), energy saving (e.g., Cialdini 2003), and voting (e.g., Gerber and Green 2000; Gerber and Rogers 2009; Gerber and Rogers 2009; Glynn, Huge, and Lunney 2009), to name a few. The fundamental proposition guiding this program of research is that perceptions of social norms are positively related to behaviors that are consistent with this norm. For example, people who report, or are told, that voting is more common and likely within their referent group become more likely to vote (Gerber and Green 2000; Gerber and Rogers 2009; Glynn, Huge, and Lunney 2009).

The rich literature on social norms coupled with the promise of normative message appeals in persuasion, inspired my research project that examined the relationship between political descriptive norms on a college campus and political behaviors on that campus (Shulman and Levine 2012). If political social norms positively associate with political participation, as normative propositions suggest, then future work can focus on creating messages that intend to increase perceptions of political social norms within that environment. With this logic in mind, our study tested whether normative perceptions were a viable motivator of political activity within this demographic. Moreover, consistent with Dalton's (2008) work, by using other Millennials as a normative referent, instead of Americans in general, the link between citizenship norms and political behavior may be more apparent and more pronounced.

In order to test the relationship between normative perceptions and behaviors on college campuses, this study analyzed data from 32 different college campuses across the United States via an online survey (N = 1,389; for more information, see Shulman and Levine 2012). Interestingly, it was revealed that students on the same campus report similar perceptions of social norms relative to students on other campuses (intraclass correlation of 0.29). This finding notably demonstrates that perceptions of political social norms exist beyond the individual-level of analysis and vary by environment. This environmental variation potentially illustrates Dalton's (2008) finding that Millennials are more attuned to proximal norms than they are to national norms. Given the variability of political norms by social environment, targeting college students through more immediate social norms (e.g., students at their own college or possibly even within their classroom) makes theoretical and empirical sense.

In addition to specifying the variability of different environmental norms, additional analyses were ran using hierarchical linear modeling (Hayes 2006; Hox 2002; Raudenbush and Bryk 2001) to test whether perceptions of social norms at the group-level, and within one's social environment (i.e., college campus), predicted actual political participation at the individual-level. Consistent with normative theory, this relationship held with our data. Specifically, perceptions of norms at the group-level positively predicted political participation at the individual-level (b = 0.12, SE = 0.06, t (30) = 2.04, p = 0.05). This finding demonstrates that cultivating political social norms at the group-level, and using one's fellow college students as a referent, does account for—at least partially—college students' political behavior.

What follows from this exciting finding is the question of how political social norms can be cultivated? In addition to measuring social norms and political participation, we also measured interpersonal political communication. Our reason for doing so was to test whether normative perceptions could be accounted for by the frequency of political conversation within that environment (Lapinski and Rimal 2005). The data we obtained were consistent with this notion. Using Hierarchical Linear Modeling, our work demonstrated that frequency of political conversations on campus were a significant and positive predictor of normative perceptions ($b = 0.24$, $SE = 0.06$, $t(30) = 3.68$, $p < 0.001$).

Intervention Possibilities

On the whole, research guided by social norms provides insight into how to induce the motivation to participate for young audiences and from a communication perspective. This insight can be applied by administrators or politicians looking to change the normative culture at the institutional level. At the local level, changes to normative culture can be instigated by teachers and educators in the classroom. In the classroom, normative theory suggests that educators would be well advised to allow students to choose the political issues that are discussed or investigated in class. Although it is common for teachers to introduce political issues because of the timeliness of the issue or the issue's prominence in national discourse, recall that Millennials are motivated by a sense of ownership, not obligation. Thus, it may be helpful for instructors to ask the class what issues they find interesting about local or national-level politics. By allowing students to set the agenda, there should be an increased likelihood of students becoming engaged with the material. Moreover, if fellow students appear interested in a particular topic, social norm propositions dictate that other students will follow suit.

At the institutional level, guided by the normative component from Delli Carpini's (2000) model, this work suggests that future campaign initiatives should look to universities to host civic engagement programs to help complement more generalized engagement campaigns that look to target this demographic (e.g., "Vote or Die" or "Rock the Vote," Payne, Hanlon, Twomey 2007). For example, if I were interested in promoting political participation at Ohio State University, I could create messages such as "Buckeyes Vote!" or "Did you know 75% of Buckeyes voted in the last election? Register to vote!" (note: the percentage was made up just for this example, regrettably this is likely a high estimate). This approach is consistent with social influence campaigns in other domains (e.g., prevent binge drinking) predicated on the social norms approach (Berkowitz 2004). A message of this kind should personalize political activity, via social norms and a shared, meaningful social referent, and in doing so increase perceptions of normative activity on campus. Our research coupled with Delli Carpini's (2000) theorizing suggests that increasing these perceptions should eventually serve to increase political participation via bolstering the motivation component of his model.

A third communication-based intervention strategy inspired by the motivation deficiency from Delli Carpini's model could be to create an environment where political talk is promoted and encouraged. This intervention strategy is empirically justifiable given our finding (Shulman and Levine 2012) that the frequency of political talk on campus positively relates to perceptions of political norms. One communication-based approach to employ this strategy would be that in addition to creating messages such as "Buckeyes Vote," organizational structures within the university could also identify ways to promote political talk through campus initiatives. For example, the student union or local restaurants could host political discussion or political trivia nights, campuses could host events where political groups on campus try to solicit new members, or universities could spend more energy trying to bring politicians to campus. Another, more out of the box idea, would be to facilitate political discussions on campus through pre-existing campus activities such as orientation visits. It is not unusual that during the orientation process, students are required to sit through a short seminar or group discussion on issues related to college students. Some of these discussion topics include maintaining a healthy lifestyle and being safe on campus. Given that during a student's time at college they become able to vote for the first time, introducing college students to the world of political thought through already existing programs could be a valuable community service that is still in line with university objectives.

Another approach is to encourage teachers and/or professors to have more in-class discussion about politics. If more teachers on campus identify political communication skills as a learning objective, the cultivation of political norms would be reinforced through multiple-channels, thus increasing the likelihood of success. These are just a few ideas, prompted by theory and research, where communication could be used to motivate political engagement through increasing perceptions of citizenship norms on campus.

Political Efficacy

Aside from motivation inspired by a sense of civic duty, motivation also can be derived from a sense of political efficacy. Political efficacy is defined as "an individual's feeling that s/he has the ability to influence the political process" (Campbell, Gurin, and Miller 1954). Political efficacy is considered one of the most important indicators of democratic health because for participation to occur in rates that are broadly representative, citizens need to buy into their system and feel that participation is worth their time (Nabatchi 2010). As a testament to the importance of efficacy, a measure has been included within the National Elections Survey (ANES) question battery since 1952. From the ANES survey, research has demonstrated that the construct of political efficacy is actually composed of two distinct dimensions labeled as external and internal political efficacy (Acock, Clarke, and Stewart 1985; Clarke and Acock

1989; Kaid, McKinney, and Tedesco 2007). According to Niemi, Craig, and Mattei (1991) external efficacy is defined as "beliefs about the responsiveness of governmental authorities and institutions to citizen's demands" (1407). In other words, this form of efficacy refers to perceptions of whether the system actually works, or put differently, whether behaviors such as voting, protests, rallies, and petitioning can actually affect change at the legislative level of government. Niemi et al. (1991) define internal political efficacy as "beliefs about one's own competence to understand, and to participate effectively, in politics" (1407). More specifically, this measure gauges participants' confidence in their ability to understand, and effectively engage in, the political process (Holbert et al. 2007; Kaid, McKinney, and Tedesco 2007).

Research examining political efficacy rates for Millennials forecasts a troubling future for American democracy. With regard to external political efficacy, research by Rahn (1998) revealed that less than 20 percent of 19–29-year-olds reported being "very proud" of US democracy. This proportion is even more disheartening when one considers that this percentage is over 30 percent lower than respondents aged 50 and older responding to the same question. Additionally, research from an organization called Campus Compact, a coalition of over 1,100 college and university presidents, in 1999 reported, "…(college) students are not connected to the larger purposes and aspirations of the American democracy. Voter turnout is low. Feelings that political participation will not make any difference are high. Added to this there is a profound sense of cynicism and lack of trust in the political process" (Basehart and Nagler 2009, 10). A similar trend is apparent for internal political efficacy. For example, 70 percent of US teenagers report no interest in a job related to politics or government (Delli Carpini 2000). This disinterest coupled with generalized cynicism toward American democracy is one reason why there is a deficiency in Millennials' political motivations.

This work implies that Millennials are in dire need of a confidence boost both in America and within themselves. In order to address this concern, it becomes important to rethink the way politics is communicated to Millennials. In this vein, I will now turn toward a research project that attempted to improve Millennials' perception of their internal political efficacy through the language used on public opinion questionnaires (Shulman, Vallesky, Solus, and Bray 2013). Internal political efficacy was chosen as our outcome measure because changing attitudes about oneself should be easier than changing one's attitudes about the larger political system. This is due to the proximal nature of the information required to affect internal efficacy relative to external efficacy, and also due to our hope that if we can change one's personal relationship with politics, this reinvigorated interest might eventually transfer to improvements in external political efficacy as well.

Why would a person believe that they are unable to understand political issues and political affairs? Although there are likely several explanations, only two come to mind here. The first reason is that this person does not consider themselves very intelligent. For whatever reason, they believe that they are unable to sufficiently grasp political information. Although some people are self-deprecating, this explanation strikes me as unlikely because more often than not people are likely to over-report their abilities in a variety of domains (i.e., self-deceptive enhancement, Paulhus 1998; Shulman and Boster 2014b). Take for example phenomena such as optimistic bias, the third-person effect, self-deceptive enhancement, and social desirability biases. What all of these concepts have in common is an abundance of research that reveals under certain conditions, people are more prone to report having abilities that are above average (or at the very least average) than below average (Lalwani, Shrum, and Chiu 2009; Paulhus et al. 2003; Paulhus 1998; Shulman and Boster 2014b; Tourangeau and Yan 2007). Therefore, the idea that internal political efficacy is low due to a person's admitted lack of self-confidence seems unlikely and inconsistent with data on self-report biases.

The second, and in my opinion more likely explanation of low internal political efficacy reports is that elite political communication is poorly crafted and poorly disseminated. Millennials may be reporting substandard levels of political efficacy because message-makers are not designing messages that adequately speak to this generation. If political messaging were improved, perhaps political efficacy reports could be improved as well. If this reasoning holds, the next question becomes how can political messages more effectively target this generation?

One limitation Millennials possess with regard to politics is a lack of political information (Craig and Maggiotto 1982; Shulman and Boster 2014b; Wilkinson 1996; Zukin et al. 2006). Because Millennials lack this information, it is often the case that when political policy is being discussed (i.e., The Dream Act) Millennials tune out because they lack familiarity of the topic and as such choose to disregard this information on the grounds of irrelevancy. Another way of theorizing about this problem is that Millennials have no attitudes that are accessible regarding a topic that they know nothing about. Although Millennials might fail to recognize the connection between public policy and their own value systems, this disconnect may be remedied through strategic changes to the way we communicate about politics. Rather than discuss formal policy, political information can be communicated in a way that makes familiar concepts more accessible. By explaining specific policy details, for example, attitudes may become more accessible regarding the issue and Millennials might become able to register an opinion on the issue and engage in a worthwhile political discussion. For example, take the Dream Act. Rather than discuss immigration policy in terms of the Dream Act, what if newscasters or pollsters began with a one-sentence description of this policy such as "An act where citizenship is granted to the child of an illegal immigrant if that child agrees to attend college or join the military." With this description in place, a person new to politics may now have more accessible attitudes on this topic and moreover, might be able to engage in a cogent discussion on this issue. By making topics more accessible by using terms and ideas that are more familiar to politically less aware constituencies, this communication strategy can promote a heightened sense of internal political efficacy.

We decided to test the viability of this communication strategy using a public opinion survey experiment. We chose a public opinion survey as our cover story and manipulation because, first, college students are well accustomed to taking a variety of surveys for their courses. A survey was also an appropriate channel to test our predictions because it has been well documented that question wording on public opinion surveys can impact the opinions espoused on these surveys (e.g., Rasinski 1989; Schwarz 1999). Given the power of survey language we tested whether survey wording could be utilized to induce higher levels of internal political efficacy. We hypothesized that subtle changes to public opinion questions would affect subsequent reports of internal political efficacy in college students, the very population that has been shown to register low ratings of internal political efficacy. In order to test this supposition, we randomly assigned participants to one of two survey conditions ($N = 90$). In one condition, language that made political policies inaccessible, or unfamiliar, was employed. For example, in the inaccessible condition, we asked students, "To what extent do you agree with Arizona's new immigration policy." Another example includes, "The government should reduce the federal deficit by reducing their spending on entitlement programs." These questions represent, or exemplify the problematic relationship between those new to politics and elite rhetoric. These questions assume that participants know about these policies. When participants aren't familiar with these terms, laws, or policies, they are likely to feel disenfranchised and should report lower levels of political efficacy. Conversely, in the accessible condition, all questions were reworded to include information and terms that intended to familiarize students with the issue. These questions do not assume knowledge, but rather provide the information needed by the participant to competently answer the question. For example, "To what do you agree with Arizona's immigration law that allows police to ask a person to verify their citizenship upon request." Or, "The government should reduce the federal deficit by reducing their spending on programs such as welfare, food stamps, and Medicare/Medicaid." Results from this study showed that, consistent with our expectations, students in the accessible question condition reported significantly higher levels of internal political efficacy ($M = 4.20$, $SD = 1.18$) than students in the inaccessible condition [$M = 3.73$, $SD = 1.08$, $t(89) = 1.99$, $p = 0.05$, $d = 0.42$].

Intervention Possibilities

This finding underscores the importance of how we communicate about politics with people who are generally uninformed. By prioritizing language that is more accessible, not only might we get more accurate opinion data, but we also might improve perceptions of political efficacy which is a key motivator of future political participation. It is worthy of note that, troublingly, many of the questions used in the inaccessible condition were taken from widely used public opinion surveys such as PEW and the American National Election Studies. This is particularly troubling given that this survey data is ostensibly trying to generate accurate reports of public opinion. However, by using language that is inaccessible or unfamiliar to certain blocs of voting eligible citizens, these surveys may inadvertently be encouraging guessing (Mondak 2001). Moreover, in addition to asking participants for responses on issues they presume to know nothing about, our data suggest that these polls may also be adversely affecting the internal political efficacy of less knowledgeable constituencies.

Similarly counterproductive processes may also be operating in the classroom. If political issues are brought up in a way that assumes knowledge or history of a given event, students with no prior knowledge of the issue might disengage. One of the challenges and opportunities for educators is to continually make new information accessible to students. Students encounter new ideas every day and are asked to retain this knowledge, recite this information, and articulate their attitudes on the subject. When this information is not worded in an optimal way, students might view this retention as a chore and as an exercise in memorization rather than an exercise in argumentation. Instructors who can convey the *idea*s or underlying values inherent in a political issue, without requiring gains to students' vocabularies in the process, should find that students will engage more with the issue, feel more confident in their opinions on the issue, and as shown in Shulman et al. (2013) find the discussion more interesting. These positive effects are achievable through small changes to the message, not changes to the curriculum. This is what makes communication so important throughout the learning process.

In sum, our findings highlight some important considerations when communicating about politics and trying to bolster the motivation component of Delli Carpini's (2000) model. Namely that it is necessary to carefully consider how we communicate about politics particularly with unaware or disinterested constituencies. If the language used in political messages reinforces participants' lack of political knowledge and awareness, it is no surprise that this reminder might cause participants to feel even more removed or alienated from the political world (e.g., participants in the inaccessible condition); conversely, if language is strategically crafted to introduce familiar terms and brief descriptors into these messages, perhaps people will feel invited rather than snubbed by the political process. This recommendation can be helpful for educators, scholars, or practitioners. Additionally, our research implies that one intervention strategy in this vein could be administered through public opinion polling. Perhaps future research initiatives can work alongside these far-reaching polling organizations to create questions that instill their survey respondents with greater political efficacy while also potentially improving the quality of their opinion data.

TARGETING PERCEPTIONS OF MILLENNIALS' POLITICAL ABILITIES

Overview

Referring back to Delli Carpini's (2000) model of engagement, our attention now turns to deficiencies rooted in the *abilities* domain. Examples of these abilities include: time, money, information, and certain kinds of organizational, communication, and leadership skills. According to Delli Carpini, with respect to these ability types, the greatest barrier to entry with Millennials in particular is lack of information. As a testament to this knowledge deficiency, only 10 percent of people between the ages of 19–29 can name both of their senators (Delli Carpini 2000). More recently we found in our college student sample that students answered an average of 7.49 questions correctly on an open-ended 23 question political knowledge test (33% correct; Shulman and Boster 2014b). Despite a sizable dearth in political knowledge and information, an intervention strategy that aims to immediately remedy information deficiencies may be short-sighted. Being consistently aware of political happenings is a life-long endeavor. Although it may be beneficial in the short term to teach Millennials about current political issues, eventually these issues will become outdated alongside the information intervention. Instead it will be argued here that intervention strategies that aim to improve communication skills may be better suited to facilitate long-term political engagement. And by developing political abilities at a young age, these audiences have a higher likelihood of being politically engaged later in life (Aldrich, Montgomery, and Wood 2011; Collins, Kumar, and Bendor 2009; Denny and Doyle 2009; Plutzer 2002). The types of abilities I am referring to include how to effectively and successfully discuss politics with others, how to communicate about politics in more captivating and interesting ways, and how to seek out credible political information in a vast communication landscape. The possession of these skills will well equip younger audiences to engage with politics throughout their lifetime.

Given that this type of intervention strategy is rooted in cultivating interest, knowledge, and communication abilities within younger audiences, it is logical that most of the strategies used to promote these skills occur within an educational context. Through civics curricula students can learn basic information about political processes (thus improving the knowledge and information dimensions), while also gaining experience talking about these processes through classroom discussion (communications dimension). To this end, there have been a few notable studies undertaken in the field of communication that assessed classroom efforts that aimed at improving students' political abilities and in doing so endeavored to promote long-term political engagement.

One example of these efforts is Kids Voting USA, an initiative geared toward "envision[ing] the school as an organized setting for the practice and development of skills important to citizenship" (McDevitt and Chaffee 2000: 4). Although research tends to focus on the effectiveness of civic education programs for improving students' political knowledge, communication theorists have shifted their focus toward whether these programs improve political communication abilities. For example, McDevitt and Chaffee's (2000) work hypothesized that exposure to Kids Vote USA would increase political discussions within the household (between students and parents), increase frequency of newspaper reading and TV news viewing, increase attention to campaign news, and ultimately serve to increase election knowledge. Consistent with their expectations, the results of their study found that while exposure to a civic education program did slightly improve knowledge (actually knowledge was the smallest gain), the greatest gains were obtained in students' political communication abilities.

After conducting a series of studies on the effects of Kids Voting USA, McDevitt and Kiousis (2006) developed their Deliberative Learning Model (DLM) to synthesize the learning processes they observed through the Kids Vote program. The DLM is predicated on the idea that political engagement strengthens as interpersonal political discussions become (1) more frequent, and (2) include a greater diversity of communication partners. Their primary thesis is that civic education serves to stimulate initial political discussions and spark early political interest; in doing so these programs put the political learning model in motion.

According to the McDevitt and Kiousis's (2006) model, political learning can be tracked along three stages of development. A participant moves from stage to stage through the diffusion of interpersonal discussion. According to the authors:

> ...[the DLM] departs from conventional views of civic education evaluation in its emphasis on the diffusion of interpersonal political communication from schools to families and adolescent peer groups. The diffusion allows for the induction of habitual discussion and opinion refinement within the primary groups that are arguably most consequential for adolescents' civic development. (248)

Thus, what is impactful about civic education curricula is not necessarily the lessons learned through the intervention (though this helps), but actually the communication opportunities provided through these initiatives. According to the McDevitt and Kiousis (2006), traditional perspectives on civic education tend to adopt the "transmission" model. This model assumes that students passively absorb political information taught in class. The transmission model focuses on individual-level cognition and behavior such as information gain. By contrast, the DLM posits that civic education curricula also promotes relational learning. Through discussion opportunities in the classroom, students slowly develop confidence in their ability to express political opinions and learn how to communicate interpersonally about politics in polite and constructive ways (McDevitt and Kiousis 2006). These initial classroom discussions constitute the first stage of the DLM, termed "peer-centered communication in school," wherein students practice discussing politics with a group of peers who are at the same level of political development.

The second stage of the DLM is called the "diffusion of deliberative inclinations." In this stage students transition from extrinsic motivations for political learning (e.g., grade in class) to intrinsic motivations such as general interest, information gain, and opinion expression. Participants who grow into this stage of political development will begin to engage in spontaneous political interactions and information-seeking outside of the classroom. Although it is most likely that these behaviors are first introduced in the household (McLeod and Chaffee 1972; McDevitt and Chaffee 2000; Shulman and DeAndrea 2014a), eventually these discussions may begin to occur in other contexts as well. Once political discussions begin to consistently occur beyond the classroom, the third stage of the DLM is achieved: "receptivity to future learning." With communication abilities in place, participants are equipped to engage within the political system for the long term. At this stage participants have the confidence, skills, and wherewithal to understand the political system and their role within it (Moy et al. 2004).

McDevitt and Kiousis's (2006) model proffers that positive experiences with political discussions in the classroom may serve to stimulate future political discussions outside the classroom. What remains to be considered however is whether there is a certain style of communication that improves the probability for success within this model? As such, the focus of Shulman and Wittenbaum (2013) was to identify specific communication styles that associate with positive political experiences.

For this study we recruited 162 undergraduate students via the communication research pool. This procedure highlights important distinctions between our research and the aforementioned studies on civic education because in our study we recruited people to engage in a political discussion for research credits—not for class, not within a broader curriculum, and not for a grade. Although it is sensible that students would be more motivated to discuss politics when they are being graded on their ability to do so, the possibility that similar outcomes can be achieved under the guise of academic research is less costly and therefore promising. With regard to their group discussion, we tested the presence or absence of two opposing styles of communication. We hypothesized that higher levels of cooperative communication would be associated with more positive outcomes, whereas higher levels of adversarial communication would be negatively associated with positive outcomes.

Our data revealed that, consistent with expectations, communication style did impact perceptions of knowledge gain $[F (2, 153) = 3.01, p = 0.052, \text{Adj. } R^2 = 0.03]$ and decision satisfaction $[F (2, 159) = 89.61, p < 0.01, \text{Adj. } R^2 = 0.06]$. Specifically, when knowledge gained was the dependent variable, both cooperative communication, $b = 0.23, SE = 0.18, t = 2.06, p < 0.05$, and adversarial communication, $b = 0.26, SE = 0.16, t = 2.40, p < 0.05$, emerged as significant and positive predictors of knowledge gain. Although this direction was expected in the case of cooperative communication, the fact that an adversarial style similarly associated with these positive outcomes was unexpected. When decision satisfaction was the dependent variable, again both cooperative communication, $b = 0.49, SE = 0.10, t = 5.78, p < 0.05$, and adversarial communication, $b = -0.28, SE = 0.10, t = -3.25, p < 0.05$, emerged as significant predictors. Moreover, for these analyses, these coefficients supported study hypotheses such that cooperative communication positively associated with knowledge and satisfaction, whereas adversarial communication was negatively associated only in the case of decision satisfaction.

Although Shulman and Wittenbaum (2013) demonstrated the benefits of having political discussions with peers (even in formal or contrived contexts), the question remains as to how long these effects last? In other words, if the intervention is short-lived, are the effects short-lived as well? To answer this question, some recent research I conducted helped to empirically address this question.

In our study (Shulman et al. 2014) we collected measures of political interest (a measure pertinent to the *abilities* dimension via Delli Carpini 2000) and political efficacy (*motivation* dimension) at three different time points over the duration of ten weeks. We initially sent out emails to everyone in the participant pool with a link to our pretest survey ($N = 104$). Two weeks later these participants participated in three-person, ad hoc political discussion (students did not know their discussion partners, $n = 74$). Three weeks following these discussions, students were asked to take the final survey. Our intention with this research design was to assess both the short-term and long-term impact of political group discussion on outcomes related to the abilities and motivation components of Delli Carpini's model (2000).

What we found, consistent with expectations for interest $F (2, 112) = 8.34$, $p < 0.05$, and efficacy, $F (2, 96) = 7.07$, $p < 0.05$, was that reports of interest (pretest: $M = 3.67$, $SD = 1.68$) and efficacy (pretest: $M = 3.47$, $SD = 1.33$) increased immediately following the group discussion (postdiscussion: interest: $M = 3.83$, $SD = 1.57$; efficacy: $M = 3.63$, $SD = 1.31$). This finding is encouraging in its demonstration that practice and experience with political communication improves perceptions of politics (i.e., politics is more interesting than I thought) and abilities (i.e., I am better at understanding politics than I once thought). This work, thus far, corroborates some of the studies previously discussed. In order to extend our understanding, however, and following from the DLM (McDevitt and Kiousis 2006), it is important to consider whether this positive political experience sustains over time. Research has shown that people who score highly on political interest and political efficacy also discuss politics more frequently and are more likely to politically participate (Delli Carpini, Cook, and Jacobs 2004). Thus, if higher reports of interest and efficacy persist three weeks following the discussion, we can be hopeful that the observed gains in interest and efficacy may also promote more frequent political discussions moving forward.

We were pleased to see that our results suggest that political interest (postdiscussion: $M = 3.83$, $SD = 1.57$) and political efficacy (postdiscussion: $M = 3.63$, $SD = 1.31$) not only sustain over time but actually increase (posttest: interest: $M = 4.18$, $SD = 1.66$; efficacy: $M = 3.88$, $SD = 1.46$). It is important to mention that this finding cannot be attributed to panel, or practice effects, because students who participated in the discussion compared with students who did not [$n = 27$; because other participants were no-shows), were more likely to report higher levels of internal political efficacy, $F(2, 148) = 5.53$, $p < 0.05$ (but not political interest, $F(2, 164) = 0.62$, $p = 0.538$].

Intervention Possibilities

There are a few important implications derived from this research. The first is that, overall, cooperative communication was a stronger and more reliable predictor of positive political outcomes. Building off of Delli Carpini's (2000) model, along with McDevitt and Kiousis's work (2006), this finding suggests that it is not the mere presence of communication that promotes positive political experiences. Instead, attention must be paid toward specific communication behaviors that help bolster desirable outcomes. From this study, we can identify a couple of strategies to improve perceptions of college students' political abilities. The first regards training students on how to talk about politics. If instructions were given in the classroom, before meetings, or wherever else political discussions occur, that impressed upon participants the importance of listening, respectful dialogue, and patience—perhaps even stronger positive outcomes could arise from these opportunities. A second take away from this research is that political discussions, even without a formal initiative, can still yield some of the beneficial effects obtained in other, more time-intensive, research. This latter finding does not intend to downplay the effects attained from civic education research, but instead suggests that educators or practitioners should take advantage opportunities—however brief—to stimulate political discussions. Our work demonstrates that, particularly when communication is cooperative, beneficial outcomes can still be produced.

In sum, this work illustrates that political group discussions function to not only improve knowledge gain and decision satisfaction (Shulman and Wittenbaum 2013), but also increase internal political efficacy, and to a lesser extent political interest (Shulman et al. 2014). Moreover, this effect appears to sustain over time despite the relatively short (20 minutes) discussion period. This constitutes an exciting finding because it suggests that initiating political discussions, even short ad hoc discussions, can be a fruitful engagement strategy. Educators, for example, could utilize classroom time by having students engage in small group discussions about current political issues. If our findings hold, these short, classroom discussions could lead to important gains in knowledge, satisfaction, efficacy, and interest. Another strategy that could be employed based on the aforementioned logic is to include political discussions as part of research opportunities typically offered as extra credit in college courses. This latter example provides an opportunity for students to talk about politics, while also allowing researchers to study these processes in an effort to learn how these discussions can be engineered to be even more effective.

Taken together, this work underscores the importance of facilitating a peer-centered learning environments for younger audiences. Regardless of whether these discussions were formal, informal, short, long, graded, or ungraded, they still seem to produce positive political outcomes within discussion participants. As such, continuing to find venues and excuses to incorporate political discussions into everyday life should be considered an efficient and effective communication-based intervention strategy in the promotion of civic engagement.

Targeting Millennials' Political Opportunity

Overview

The final barrier Delli Carpini (2000) refers to is the *opportunity* dimension. More specifically, "Opportunities are determined by the civic infrastructure: from the structure and processes of elections to the number and type of civic organizations" (344). This dimension is akin to reasoning from Verba, Schlozman, and Brady's (1995) Civic Volunteerism Model in which the authors posit that one reason people do not become involved in politics is because no one asked. Because Millennials are not being readily invited into the political process, Delli Carpini (2000) and Verba, Schlozman, and Brady (1997) argue that, similar to other underrepresented populations, these groups feel disenfranchised and ignored from the political system. Although elites may argue that ignoring Millennials is justified, because they do not vote and are generally unaware and uninformed of political happenings, theorists concerned with unequal representation would retort that more aggressive efforts are needed to pursue these demographics in the first place. Groups of people who are systematically ignored become quickly disillusioned with the political process. These feelings reflect Millennials' distrust in the system (external political efficacy), and constitute a cause for concern. As such, it becomes important to consider systematic ways to invite people into the political process, preferably through trusted and local institutions whose solicitation requests would be more likely to be accepted.

In Verba, Schlozman, and Brady's (1995) initial theorizing on this issue, it was argued that membership in voluntary organizations (e.g., church groups, charitable groups, political organizations, sports teams, etc.) facilitates political participation. The reason these groups, regardless of type, facilitate political action is because through exposure to more people, solicitation requests for political activity becomes more probable. Not only do solicitation requests become more probable, but they are also more likely to be accepted than requests from unacquainted sources. This is because known sources are more similar and trusted, thus rendering influence attempts more successful.

Despite the promise of using one's group membership as a conduit to promote political activity, this strategy is not often implemented beyond civic education programs in high school. The paucity of these types of programs at the college-level is particularly unfortunate for several reasons. For one, college-aged students can vote. Moreover, given that it is this group's first time doing so, reminding them of the political process at a time when this information is highly relevant should be very helpful. Additionally, many students identify with other students at their college, making appeals from other students at their university possibly more successful. College campuses are also large, so the cost of these interventions might not be so considerable when taking into account the number of students occupying a relatively small area. These students also have access to common locations and are exposed to relatively similar messaging via university message boards, email systems, TV access, and so on. Altogether these features suggest civic intervention programs implemented within one's university might be both successful and efficient if correctly applied. This premise leads to the final study that will be discussed in this chapter. This relatively new research begins to consider how to utilize structures within the college campus to promote activity (Shulman and Chod 2015).

This work was guided by both short-term and long-term objectives. In the short term, our goal was to try and identify why some college campuses are "more political than others." With this understanding in place, over time we could then consider our second, and more strategic objective, which is to figure out how to replicate these features at less political institutions. Unfortunately, however, when looking for guidance on how to begin investigating these objectives, we were struck by how little research actually describes features or characteristics of politicized environments. Given the paucity of research that has attempted to identify shared characteristics between politicized environments, our work aimed to answer this question. By understanding similarities between politicized contexts, perhaps light could be shed on why these environments are more successful at mobilizing their student body, and future work may be better informed of how to replicate these desirable outcomes.

With these short-term and long-term goals in mind, we (Shulman and Chod 2015) reanalyzed the data from Shulman and Levine's (2012) multicampus study. This dataset allowed us to begin addressing the aforementioned objectives in that we were able to compare the same measures of political activity (frequency of political communication and political participation) across several different social contexts (university campuses). Although we do not intend to attribute causality to any of the relationships we uncovered below, we do believe that the insights afforded by this relatively unique dataset and methodology warrant consideration as we attempt to uncover what makes institutions political.

There were a few key results obtained from our data. First, we observed that there was a strong positive relationship between university rejection rate, political participation $r(37) = 0.41$, $p < 0.01$, and frequency of political talk, $r(37) = 0.44$, $p < 0.001$. This relationship reveals that political participation and talk is more frequent at selective universities (for a list of universities, see Shulman and Levine 2012). In terms of the other features, we observed that region of the country (West and Northeast) and institution type (private v public) associated significantly with political participation and political talk, such that political activity was lowest at Midwestern universities (participation: $M = 4.20$, $SD = 0.56$; talk: $M = 2.57$, $SD = 0.33$) and highest at Western universities in the case of participation [$M = 5.15$, $SD = 0.75$, $F(3, 35) = 3.71$, $p < 0.05$, $\eta^2 = 0.24$], and highest at Northeastern universities in the case of political talk [$M = 3.33$, $SD = 1.15$, $F(3, 35) = 2.79$, $p = 0.055$, $\eta^2 = 0.19$]. It was also found that both political participation [$t(37) = 2.92$, $p < 0.05$, $d = 0.96$, $r = 0.43$] and political talk [$t(37) = 1.87$, $p = 0.07$, $d = 0.61$, $r = -0.29$] was more frequent at private schools versus public schools. Interestingly, we also found that there was a positive relationship that approached statistical significance between political diversity on campus and political participation, $r(37) = 0.28$, $p = 0.08$, and political communication, $r(37) = 0.22$, $p = 0.174$.

Intervention Possibilities

This research is in its formative stages of development, so the intervention strategies implied by our findings are not yet crystallized. To make matters more ambiguous, our data was underpowered so we had to rely on statistical trends and effect sizes for interpretation. Nevertheless, given the size of these estimates, we believe that we have a good starting point for making sense of the relationships we uncovered in this study.

First, we found that selective campuses in urban or populated locations (based on the campuses located in the West and Northeast) were more likely to have politically active students. Moreover, political activity was more likely at private institutions relative to public institutions. With these findings in place, we can begin to speculate about how to explain these findings. One explanation may be that private schools are more likely to have resources that facilitate political activity compared to public schools. Another plausible explanation may be that exposure to political diversity on campus actually promotes political engagement and motivates political activity through more engaging political discussions. Despite the speculative nature of these explanations, it is hoped that future experimental work may be better able to uncover the motivations behind our findings. Doing so could implicate how to create environments that promote political activity by creating opportunities for its residents to politically participate.

Conclusion

The purpose of this chapter was to consider communication-based intervention strategies that could be used to combat the political hurdles experienced by Millennials. It has been advanced that using social norm messages to increase perceptions of political activity on campus may be one strategy that inevitably leads to actual participation. It was also proposed that when talking about politics, either through campaigns, public opinion surveys, or within classroom discussions, it is paramount to make sure that the language being used makes political attitudes as accessible as possible. By making attitudes accessible through language, participants feel more confident in their abilities to express their political opinions. Moreover, these subtle changes to language might also function to make politics more interesting to politically unaware constituencies. These intervention strategies were specifically geared toward addressing Delli Carpini's (2000) *motivation* component.

In order to remedy what Delli Carpini (2000) refers to as deficiencies in *ability*, our research showed that involving students in peer-centered political discussions can be one strategy to combat shortcomings in information and political communication skills. Through practice, first in controlled settings such as a classroom or research study, students can gain experience, confidence, and the information required for thinking about politics, while also practicing how to best express their opinions with others. What we learned from our research (Shulman and Wittenbaum 2013) was that there should be a particular emphasis on how people are talking politics. Future engagement campaigns or educational initiatives should make it clear that while discussing politics, certain communication traits such as listening, patience, and respect (i.e., cooperative communication) should be implemented in order to make these discussions as effective as possible.

Finally, this work began to consider how to explain, structurally, features of environments that promote political activity. There was a suggestion in all the research presented that improving the frequency of political communication, either at one's college campus or in their classroom, can increase the political participation of young people. One way to potentially promote political communication may be to create opportunities that highlight the diverse range of political opinions that exist on-campus. Our most recent work (Shulman and Chod 2015) indicates that political diversity is positively related to increased political discussion and participation. If this holds, creating events that highlight differences of opinions on campus may function to energize and mobilize this constituency.

To conclude, this chapter was meant to question an important assumption that often goes unconsidered in Millennial engagement research. Rather than blaming Millennials for their dearth of knowledge and political action, perhaps the blame should be shared by media, elites, educators, and institutions that have failed to adequately invite Millennials into the political process. Politics begins and ends with some form of communication. By rethinking how we, as scholars, practitioners, and educators, can use communication to our advantage, we can create novel messages and employ novel strategies to improve the representativeness of American democracy, beginning with Millennials.

References

Acock, Alan, Harold D. Clarke, and Marianne C. Stewart. 1985. "A New Model for Old Measures: A Covariance Structure Analysis of Political Efficacy." *Journal of Politics* 47 (November):1062–1084.

Aldrich, John H., Jacob M. Montgomery, and Wendy Wood. 2011. "Turnout as a Habit." *Political Behavior* 4 (December): 535–563.

Almond, Gabriel A. and Sydney Verba. 1963. *The Civic Culture*. Princeton, NJ: Princeton University Press.

Basehart, Harry and Peter Nagler. 2009. "Proceedings from Presidential Citizens Scholars Program, PACE: *A New Generation, a New Engagement?*" Salisbury, MD: Salisbury University.

Berkowitz, Alan D. 2004. "The Social Norms Approach: Theory, Research, and Annotated Bibliography." *Higher Education Center for Alcohol and Other Drug Abuse and Violence Prevention. US Department of Education* (August).

Campbell, Angus, Gerald Gurin, and W. E. Miller. 1954. *The Voter Decides*. Evanston, IL: Row Peterson.

Cialdini, Robert B. 2003. "Crafting Normative Messages to Protect the Environment." *Current Directions In Psychological Science* 12 (August): 105–109.

Cialdini, Robert B., Raymond R. Reno, and Carl A. Kallgren. 1990. "A Focus Theory of Normative Conduct: Recycling the Concept of Norms to Reduce Littering in Public Places." *Journal of Personality and Social Psychology* 58 (June): 1015–1026.

Clarke, Harold D., and Alan C. Acock. 1989. "National elections and political attitudes: The Case of Political Efficacy in the 1988 National Election Study." *British Journal of Political Science* 19 (October): 551–562.

Collins, Nathan A., Sunil Kumar, and Jonathan Bendor. 2009. "The Adaptive Dynamics of Turnout." *Journal of Politics* 71 (April): 457–472.

Craig, Stephen C., and Michael A. Maggiotto. 1982. "Measuring Political Efficacy." *Political Methodology* 8 (June): 85–109.

Dalton, Russell J. 2008. "Citizenship Norms and the Expansion of Political Participation." *Political Studies* 56 (February): 76–98.

Delli Carpini, Michael X. 2000. "Gen.com: Youth, Civic Engagement, and the New Information Environment." *Political Communication* 1 (September): 341–349.

Delli Carpini, Michael X., Fay Lomax Cook, and Lawrence R. Jacobs. 2004. "Public Deliberations, Discursive Participation, and Citizen Engagement: A Review of the Empirical Literature." *Annual Review of Political Science* 7 (June): 315–344.

Delli Carpini, Michael X., and Scott Ketter. 1997. *What Americans know about Politics and Why it Matters.* New Haven, CT: Yale University Press.

Denny, Kevin and Orla Doyle. 2009. "Does Voting History Matter? Analyzing Persistence in Turnout." *American Journal of Political Science* 53 (January): 17–35.

Gerber, Alan S., and Donald P. Green. 2000. "The Effect of a Nonpartisan Get-Out-the-Vote Drive: An Experimental Study of Leafletting." *Journal of Politics* 62(August): 846–857.

Gerber, Alan S. and Todd Rogers. 2009. "Descriptive Social Norms and Voter Motivation to Vote: Everybody's Voting and so Should You." *Journal of Politics* 71 (January): 178–191.

Glynn, Carol J., Michael E. Huge, and Carol A. Lunney. 2009. "The Influence of Perceived Social Norms on College Students' Intention to Vote." *Political Communication* 26 (February): 48–64.

Hayes, Andrew F. 2006. "A Primer on Multilevel Modeling." *Human Communication Research* 32 (November): 385–410.

Holbert, R. Lance, Jennifer L. Lambe, Anthony D. Dudo, and Kristin A. Carlton. 2007. "Primacy Effects of *The Daily Show* and National TV News Viewing: Young Viewers, Political Gratifications, and Internal Political Self-Efficacy." *Journal of Broadcasting and Electronic Media* 51 (December): 20–38.

Hox, Joop J. 2002. *Multilevel Analysis: Techniques and Applications.* Medwah, NJ: Lawrence Erlbaum.

Kaid, Lynda L., Mitchell S. McKinney, and John C. Tedesco. 2007. "Political Information Efficacy and Young Voters." *American Behavioral Scientist* 50 (May): 1093–1111.

Lalwani, Ashok K., L. J. Shrum, and Chi-yue Chiu. 2009. "Motivated Response Styles: The Role of Cultural Values, Regulatory Focus, and Self-Consciousness in Socially Desirable Responding." *Personality Processes and Individual Differences* 96 (April): 870–882.

Lapinski, Maria Knight and Rajiv N. Rimal. 2005. "An Explication of Social Norms." *Communication Theory* 15 (May): 127–147. doi: 10.1111/j.1468-2885.2005.tb00329.x.

McDevitt, Michael, and Spiro Kiousis. 2006. "Deliberative Learning: An Evaluative Approach to Interactive Civic Education." *Communication Education* 55 (July): 247–264.

McDevitt, Michael and Steven Chaffee. 2000. "Closing Gaps in Political Knowledge: Effects of a School Intervention Via Communication in the Home." *Communication Research* 27 (June): 259–292.

McLeod, Jim M. and Steven H. Chaffee. 1972. "The Construction of Social Reality." In *The Social Influence Processeses*, edited by James T. Tedeschi. Piscataway, NJ: Transaction Publishers, 50–99.

Mondak, Jeffrey J. 2001. "Developing Valid Knowledge Scales." *American Journal of Political Science* 45 (January): 224–238.

Moy, Patricia, Michael R. McCluskey, Kelley McCoy, and Margaret A. Spratt. 2004. "Political Correlates of Local News Media." *Journal of Communication* 54 (January): 532–546.

Nabatchi, Tina. 2010. "Deliberative Democracy and Citizenship: In Search of the Efficacy Effect." *Journal of Public Deliberation* 6 (December): 1–47.

Niemi, Richard G., Stephen C. Craig, and Franco Mattei. 1991. "Measuring Internal Political Efficacy in the 1988 National Election Study." *American Political Science Review* 85 (December): 1407–1413.

Park, Hee Sun, and Sandi W. Smith. 2007. "Distinctiveness and Influence of Subjective Norms, Personal Descriptive and Injunctive Norms, and Societal Descriptive and Injunctive Norms on Behavioral Intent: A case of two behaviors critical to organ donation." *Human Communication Research* 33 (April): 194–218.

Paulhus, Delroy L. 1998. "Interpersonal and Intrapsychic Adaptiveness of Trait Self Enhancement: A Mixed Blessing?" *Journal of Personality and Social Psychology* 74 (May): 1197–1208.

Paulhus, Delroy L., P. D. Harms, Bruce M. Nadine, and Daria C. Lysy. 2003. "The Over Claiming Technique: Self-Enhancement Independent of Ability." *Journal of Personality and Social Psychology* 84 (April): 890–904.

Payne, J. Gregory, John P. Hanlon, and David P. Twomey III. 2007. "Celebrity Spectacle Influence on Young Voters in the 2004 Presidential Campaign: What to Expect in 2008." *American Behavioral Scientist* 50 (May): 1239–1246.

Pinkleton, Bruce E., and Erica Weintraub Austin. 2004. "Media Perceptions and Public Affairs Apathy in the Politically Inexperienced." *Mass Communication & Society* 7 (November): 319–337.

Plutzer, Eric. 2002. "Becoming a Habitual Voter: Inertia, Resources, and Growth in Young Adulthood." *American Political Science Review* 96 (March): 41–56.

Rahn, W. 1998. "Generations and American National identity: A Data essay." Paper presented at a workship on "Communication in the Future of Democracy," in Washington, DC.

Rasinski, Kenneth A. 1989. "The Effect of Question Wording on Public Support for Government Spending." *Public Opinion Quarterly* 53 (October): 388–394.

Raudenbush, Stephan W., and Anthony S. Bryk. 2001. *Hierarchical Linear Models: Applications and Data Analysis Methods.* New York, NY: Sage Publications, Inc.

Rhodes, Nancy, et al. 2008. "Attitude and Norm Accessibility Affect Processing of Anti Smoking Messages." *Health Psychology* 27 (May): 224–232.

Rimal, Rajiv N., and Kevin Real. 2003. "Understanding the Influence of Perceived Norms on Behaviors." *Communication Theory* 13 (May): 184–203.

Rimal, Rajiv N., and Kevin Real. 2005. "How Behaviors are Influenced by Perceived Norms a Test of the Theory of Normative Social Behavior." *Communication Research* 32 (June): 389–414.

Schwarz, Norbert. 1999. "Self-Reports: How the Questions Shape the Answers." *American Psychologist* 54 (February): 93–105.

Shulman, Hillary C. and David C. DeAndrea. 2014a. "Predicting Success: Revisiting Assumptions About Family Political Socialization." *Communication Monographs* 81 (July): 386–406.

Shulman, Hillary C. and Franklin J. Boster. 2014b. "Effect of Test-Taking Venue and Response Format on Political Knowledge Tests." *Communication Methods and Measures* 8 (August): 177–189.

Shulman, Hillary C. and Gwen M. Wittenbaum. 2013. "Group Discussion that Promotes Positive Political Experiences." *Human communication* 16 (3): 121–132.

Shulman, Hillary C. and Timothy R. Levine. 2012. "Exploring Social Norms as a Group-Level Phenomenon: Do Political Participation Norms Exist and Influence Political Participation on College Campuses?" *Journal of Communication* 62 (June): 532–552.

Shulman, Hillary C. and Suzanne Chod. 2015. "A Closer Look at the Relationships between Institutions, Political Participation, and Interpersonal Political Discussions." Paper presented at the annual meeting of the International Communication Association, San Juan.

Shulman, Hillary C., Krista Vallesky, Jamie Solus, and Amber Bray. 2013. "Can Public Opinion Survey Wording Affect Internal Political Efficacy?: An Experiment." Poster presented at the annual meeting of the National Communication Association in Washington, DC.

Shulman, Hillary C., Kirsten Bushman, Emily Huizenga, Mary Ward, and Kyle Wresinski. 2014. "Can Group Discussions Be Used to Facilitate Political Interest and Efficacy in College Students?: A Longitudinal Study." Paper presented at the annual meeting of the National Communication Association in Chicago.

Tourangeau, Roger and Ting Yan. 2007. "Sensitive Questions in Surveys." *Psychological Bulletin* 135 (September): 859–883.

Verba, Sydney, Kay Lehman Schlozman, and Henry E. Brady. 1995. *Voice and Equality: Civic Volunteerism in American Politics.* Cambridge, MA: Harvard University Press.

Verba, Sydney, Kay Lehman Schlozman, and Henry E. Brady. 1997. "The Big Tilt: Participatory Inequality in America." *The American Prospect* 32 (May): 74–80.

Wilkinson, Helen. 1996. "But Will They Vote? The Political Attitudes of Young People." *Children and Society* 10 (September): 242–244.

Zukin, Cliff, Scott Keeter, Molly Andolina, Krista Jenkins, and Michael X. Delli Carpini. 2006. *A New Engagement: Political Participation, Civic Life, and the Changing American Citizen.* New York: Oxford University Press.

CHAPTER 4

Social Networking as a Pedagogical Tool: Effect of Twitter Use on Interest and Efficacy in Introductory-Level American Government Courses

Stephen M. Caliendo, Suzanne M. Chod,
William J. Muck, and Deron Schreck

According to the Center for Information and Research on Civic Learning and Engagement (CIRCLE), "Youth political engagement requires attention. Forty-five percent of young people age 18–29 voted in 2012, down from 51% in 2008." (2015). While the lack of civic engagement, efficacy, and political knowledge of young people is not a newly discovered trend, there is a renewed call by groups outside of political science, such as CIRCLE, as well as inside political science, such as the American Political Science Association, to do something about it. The Millennial generation may not socialize in bowling leagues (Putnam 1995), but Millennials do build connections and gain knowledge through the relationships they create in the virtual world. If those of us who teach political science courses accept a broadened definition of social capital, it is beneficial to incorporate technology into the classroom that helps students build that capital in a virtual world.

One of the Web 2.0 technologies that has gained prominence with the Millennials is Twitter. According to a GlobalWebIndex 2014 survey, 59 percent of Millennials have a Twitter account (Bennett 2014). Nonetheless, because Twitter is still relatively new compared to other social networking and microblogging sites, it is only more recently being incorporated into classrooms. Consequently, there has been little empirical work on Twitter as a pedagogical tool to increase engagement among college students (Gao, Luo, and Zhang 2012). While there is descriptive evidence that incorporating Twitter in the classroom can increase political knowledge, interest, and efficacy of college students, we must exercise caution in making assumptions that simply including a type of technology is the magic wand needed to solve the disengagement of the Millennials. It is a combination of an open classroom environment, students who may be predisposed to be politically interested, and the use of a technology that fosters social connectedness and information sharing. The combination of online and offline strategies might provide the best way to spur civic engagement in political science courses.

Drawing upon political science literature as well as education and technology literature, we examine the impact of Twitter use on civic engagement of college students in both face-to-face and online Introduction to American Government courses. Because of both theoretical and empirical limitations to this type of study, we do not expect that Twitter alone will cause an increase in political knowledge, efficacy, and interest. Rather, we expect to find that an infusion of Twitter into an open and dynamic classroom can help students become more civic-minded. We argue that choosing the appropriate technology to foster engagement, along with the in-class experience (both face-to-face and online) creates the best chance to increase political knowledge, efficacy, and interest in Millennials.

PREVIOUS LITERATURE

Putnam's (1995) original notion of social capital applied well to bowling leagues in the 1950s, but its application to the Millennial generation needs updating. Recent scholarship has pointed out that Putnam's social networks do not include the virtual world in which Millenials often reside (de Vreese 2007; Kavanaugh 2002; Wellman 1996). Because engaging in social networks assuages the cost of acquiring information (Leighley 1996; Rosenstone and Hansen 1993), Millennials can increase social capital while shortcutting the acquisition of knowledge, which in turn can contribute to an increase in civic engagement and political participation.

The Internet provides additional avenues for people to both engage in political discussions and increase their political information (Dahlgren 2000). With this, it may be time to redefine in some ways what political participation means. In his study of the relationship between media usage, activity of young people, and levels of political participation, de Vreese (2007) extends the more traditional definition of political participation by including "forums, polls, discussion groups, or organizing a Web site on a civic or political issue" (209). He finds that online news consumption is a strong predictor for online participation and that being part of online networks and communities are all positively related to political participation.

This finding is critically important due to the waning political interest of the Millennial generation. Galston (2004) discusses this along with information acquisition trends of the Millennial generation. "[O]nly 34% of freshmen think that keeping up with politics is important, down from 60% in 1966" and "Only 22.5% say they frequently discuss politics, down from 33%" (263). Additionally, seeking out political information from traditional media sources has significantly decreased. According to a 2012 Pew Research Center poll, "more people under 25 get news from digital (60 percent) than 'traditional' sources"

(Beaujon 2012). Moreover, there is an overall surge in the use of social media as a news source; "the number of people relying on social media as a news source doubled since 2010" (Beaujon 2012).

Although work has examined the effects of the Internet on overall political engagement (Bennett and Fielding 1999; Bimber 2001; Browning 1996; Dertouzos 1997; Grossman 1995; Johnson and Kaye 1998; Katz and Rice 2002; Morris 2000; Negroponte 1995; Norris 1999, 2001), there is little evidence that as information and technology advance, so does citizens' political engagement (Bimber 2001). Just as research has found that those who take political science courses may already be more interested in politics (Gimpel, Lay, and Schuknecht 2003), Johnson and Kaye (1998) found a similar pattern for those attracted to the Internet. However, Jennings and Zeitner (2003) assessed this further and found that "frequency of political use of the Internet was statistically insignificant for nearly all of the civic engagement indicators" (330).

Therefore, those of us who teach political science have the opportunity to use any pedagogical tool, including technology, at our disposal to foster the development of our students as active citizens. In a field such as political science, we know that the information presented in our courses can increase the amount of political knowledge our students obtain (Niemi and Junn 1998). Campbell (2008) argues that this classroom exposure introduces students to the fundamental components of our democracy, and a classroom described as having an open climate promotes political engagement. While students in political science courses may have heightened political interest as well as an increased level of comfort for political participation (Comber 2005; Gimpel, Lay, and Schuknecht 2003; Levine 2007; Niemi and Junn 1998), instructors can employ various forms of media in order to develop student attention and motivation (Seaman 1998; Bartlett and Strough 2003). One way to do this is to incorporate the Internet into the class experience.

We are now in the era of Web 2.0, which is more hands-on for the user, more cooperative among users, and more informal (Greenhow, Robelia, and Hughes 2009). Web 2.0 consists of "social digital technologies" (Palfrey and Gasser 2008, 1) such as Facebook, YouTube, Blogger, and Twitter. Research has shown students in college create an online presence in anticipation of using online social networking as a way to learn (Barnes, Marateo, and Ferris 2007; Fisher and Baird 2005). Looking at students' use of Facebook, Ellison, Steinfield, and Lampe (2007) determined that there is a positive and direct relationship between use and a feeling of social belonging. This type of belonging, albeit in a virtual world, can lend itself to an increased amount of social capital and eventual civic engagement. Using a social networking site can encourage students to learn from each other, build a community, and take a greater amount of control over their learning.

This is precisely what social constructivist theory posits. Learners become active as opposed to passive in their attempt to deconstruct the world (Eggen and Kauchak 1999) and share knowledge and information in a group setting (Dori and Belcher 2005). This can help students feel more of a part of a community, and using educational technology at the college level can foster an atmosphere for a meaningful dialogue to take place (Dori and Belcher 2005). It is critical, however, for instructors to choose the appropriate technology to foster this type of environment. Jonassen (2004) outlines eight necessary components for creating online courses. Technology used must address active, constructive, collaborative, intentional, complex, contextual, conversational, and reflective factors. These eight characteristics also can be applied in the decision to implement technology in a traditional classroom setting. Cennamo, Ross, and Ertmer (2010) address technology adoption and argue that instructors need to recognize the appropriate technology to meet learning objectives, stipulate how the technology will assist students in demonstrating learning objectives, and empower students to use the technology in the learning process (10). If we frame this in the context of Jonassen's eight components, for political science courses, in particular, the content requires that any pedagogical instrument elicit the combination of prior knowledge with new knowledge to make sense of the world (constructive), address dissonance in points-of-view on any given topic (complex), and be real-world centered (contextual). Content can be better communicated by using a technology where the student is an involved participant in the processing of information (active), uses interaction with other participants as a support system (conversational and collaborative), and internalizes factors to create a heightened understanding of political phenomena (reflective).

Taking into account both suggestions from pedagogical literature, as well as current trends in the social media use of Millennials, the question becomes: What type of Web 2.0 technology best facilitates an increase in civic engagement of college students? According to one of the first comprehensive analyses of Twitter conducted by Java et al. (2007), Twitter networks are comprised of people who have specific common interests and communicate about opinions, beliefs, and experiences. Moreover, the study categorized user intentions; a few of note are information sharing, reporting news, and information seeking (Java et al. 2007). Furthermore, Twitter is one of the most often used forms of social media to obtain news. According to the Pew Research Center's Internet and American Life Project, "15% of online adults use Twitter as of February 2012, and 8% do so on a typical day" (Smith and Brenner 2012). More importantly, "Twitter use among 18–24 year olds increased dramatically between May 2011 and February 2012, both overall and on a 'typical day' basis" (Smith and Brenner 2012). In regard to what is being shared on Twitter, over 85 percent of topics are news-related (Kwak et al. 2010). A Princeton Survey Research Associates study conducted for the Pew Research Center in January 2012 reports that as opposed to Facebook,

Twitter users' news links come from "a more even mix of family and friends and news organizations. Most of these users also felt that without Twitter they would have missed this kind of news" (Mitchell, Rosensteil, and Christian 2013). It is clear that Twitter users find news that expands their knowledge while building social networks in a virtual world, both of which contribute to increased participation in civic activities.

While there has yet to be an examination of the use of Twitter in political science classes in the context of student engagement, Junco, Heibergert, and Loken (2011) examined the effects of Twitter on student engagement and course performance for prehealth professional majors. This is the first study to specifically explore the impact of Twitter as a pedagogical facilitator of student engagement.[1] While the authors measure engagement as a function of students' relationship with class material as well as richness of academic discussions, they also found evidence that "students made connections when realizing they had shared values and interests" and "built strong relationships across diverse groups" (Junco, Heibergert, and Loken 2011: 126).

In the context of social connectedness, increased knowledge, social constructivism, and following Jonassen's recommendations for technology adoption, Twitter is an appropriate technological tool to incorporate in political science classrooms. Twitter creates an online community of people with common interests and allows users to share information in order to gain knowledge. Moreover, it requires users to be active consumers of the information, combine old and new information, provides an opportunity for users to learn from each other, exposes users to dissimilar opinions, revolves around real-world events, and provides an opportunity for users to reflect on their interactions. Nonetheless, while we can theorize that Twitter has an effect on students' political knowledge, efficacy, and interest, we must take caution in hypothesizing that this relationship is causal and positive. Because students who take political science courses are predisposed to be politically interested, and Millennials use Twitter as a means to engage in the virtual world, we expect that infusing Twitter in an open and dynamic class environment can supplement students' knowledge, engagement, and connectedness. Assessing this relationship provides the first empirical look at whether or not Twitter is a useful pedagogical tool to increase civic engagement.

ANECDOTAL BENEFITS OF USING TWITTER

We wanted to see if there was a way to get our students more civically engaged using a technology with which they were both already familiar, and that could connect students to each other and to the issues raised in class. The idea of testing the effectiveness of Twitter began with observational evaluation. We began with informal assessments of Twitter participation, without making it part of students' overall course grade. However, without incentivizing students to tweet, they were not using the technology with any regularity. Therefore, tweeting became a requirement worth 10 percent of the overall course grade. Additionally, a rubric to set expectations for students along with assessing participation was created.

Substantively, in classes where Twitter is a course requirement, the interaction between the instructors and the students on Twitter helped create a more interactive classroom environment. For instance, on a regular basis, we mention tweets from students and discuss their relevance to both the class material as well as real-world politics. This brings the virtual world into the real world. Additionally, the reverse happens when during class discussion, both the students and the instructor mention either something they read or saw and say, "I'll tweet that after class!" The translation of the connectedness online to the connectedness offline should help increase social capital.

Moreover, the attempt by the instructors to respond to every student tweet helps facilitate conversation and a deeper analysis of the issues being discussed. This is also exemplified when students respond to each other's tweets and begin a conversation. These online interactions that occur outside of class keep our "community" connected. We hope to cultivate a culture in which students regularly use Twitter as a means to build relationships, increase knowledge, and discuss politics—all of which contribute to civic engagement. While the independent effect of the inclusion of the tweets into the class discussion and Twitter conversations on civic engagement cannot be measured empirically, it prompted us to look for ways to test the use of Twitter more generally on civic engagement. We were seeing that students seemed more connected to us, to each other, and to both the material and real-world politics with the inclusion of Twitter as a course requirement. The question, though, was whether the credit should go to Twitter.

EXPERIMENTAL DESIGN

Anecdotal evidence is instructive. Part of growing as an instructor is by trial-and-error and by adopting best practices from our colleagues. Combined, we have 60 years of experience teaching at the college level, and of late we have become convinced that using Twitter provides a unique way to encourage students to stay connected to the material between class meetings. We cannot, however, know for sure what effect using Twitter is having on students' political efficacy or interest in politics unless we assess it formally, holding other factors constant. To that end, we offer the results of an experimental design intended to isolate Twitter use so that we can more adequately measure its effect.

The participants in this study are students who enrolled in an Introduction to Political Science course at a midwestern community college during the 2014 calendar year. This approach is an improvement over previous attempts (i.e., Caliendo, Chod, and Muck 2013a, b) because it maximizes the number of

Table 4.1 Portrait of participants (pretest)

Gender (N = 148)	51.4% Female
Race (N = 147)	7.5% African American 20.4% Latino/a 63.9% White 8.2% Other
Ideology (N = 147)	13.6% Extremely liberal/liberal/somewhat liberal 31.3% Neither liberal nor conservative 29.9% Extremely conservative/conservative
Party identification (N = 150)	47.3% Democratic 22.0% Republican 30.7% independent/other
Discussed politics online in week prior to pretest (N = 150)	19.3%
Mean time spent using social media (general) (N = 149)	5.40
Mean time spent using social media (discussing politics) (N = 151)	1.62

Note: Gender and race were open-ended questions. Ideology is coded from 1 (extremely liberal) to 7 (extremely conservative). Questions relating to time spent on social media were worded as follows: "On a scale of 0–10, with 0 being "never" and 10 being "many hours every day," how often would you say that you use social media to engage with others [*about politics*]?" (emphasis in original).

students while holding constant the instructor and limiting the historical context.[2] On the first day of class, students were asked to complete a pretest that contained all of the key items, as well as demographic information and information about their use of social media. Table 4.1 provides a profile of the participants at the start of the course.

Participants are evenly divided between men and women; nearly two-thirds are white. While most consider themselves to be Democrats, the ideology scale is slightly skewed toward the right. Nearly one-third of participants indicated that they were "neither liberal nor conservative," and about the same proportion do not identify with either of the two major US political parties. For 87 percent of the participants, this was the first political science course they had ever taken at the college level, and few of them were engaged in discussing politics online at the start of the course, even though they did, on average, report using social media moderately.

Measuring Interest and Efficacy

There are three key dependent variables in this study: political interest, internal efficacy, and external efficacy. We measure political interest by asking two questions borrowed from American National Election Studies surveys. The first emerged in 2006: "How interested are you in information about what's going on in government and politics?" (extremely interested, very interested, moderately interested, slightly interested, or not interested at all) (Shani 2012). We also asked the traditional item, which is worded as follows: "Some people seem to follow what's going on in government and public affairs most of the time, whether there's an election going on or not. Others aren't that interested. Would you say you follow what's going on in government and public affairs most of the time, some of the time, only now and then, or hardly at all?"

Political efficacy has been conceptualized as two discrete constructs: internal (Niemi, Craig, and Mattei 1991) and external (Chamberlain 2013; see also Dyck and Lascher 2009; Pingree 2011). Internal efficacy has been defined as "beliefs about one's own competence to understand, and to participate effectively in, politics," while external efficacy "refer[s] to beliefs about the responsiveness of governmental authorities and institutions to citizen demands" (Niemi, Craig, and Mattei 1991, 1407–1408, relying on Lane 1959). We attempt to tap into internal efficacy by way of three questions with five-point ("strongly agree" to "strongly disagree") Likert scale options: "Given the opportunity, I feel that I could do a good job influencing public officials"; "To the extent that citizens can influence politics, my efforts to do so would be more effective than the average person's"; and "Sometimes politics and government seem so complicated that a person like me can't really understand what is going on." Finally, we capture external efficacy by way of two items, also measured by five-point Likert response options: "People like me don't have any say about what the government does" and "I don't think public officials care much what people like me think." For the purpose of analysis, all items were coded or recoded so that higher values indicate greater levels of interest or efficacy. Confirmatory principal component analyses indicate that each of the three constructs are appropriately measured by the intended items.[3] Scales were conducted for the efficacy measures.[4] The differing response options do not permit simple additive indexing for the interest construct; these items will be analyzed separately.

Baseline Measures

The second column in Table 4.2 features mean responses of each item from the pretest, which was administered on the first day of class. Participants report moderate levels of all indicators, in the aggregate. The first interest item yielded a mean response slightly higher than "moderately interested"; the second item's mean falls about halfway between "some of the time" and "now and then"; and four of the five efficacy items hover right around "neither agree nor disagree." Only the second external efficacy item ("care much") sits noticeably lower, about halfway between the middle response and one response option lower. The scales, naturally, feature similar results.

Changes in Interest and Efficacy

Our first order of business is to examine how student interest and efficacy might have changed over the course of the semester. On the whole, students were more efficacious and reported more interest in government and public affairs at the end of

Table 4.2 Changes in interest and efficacy, aggregate

	Pretest (N)	Posttest, control (N)	Posttest, treatment (N)	Posttest ANOVA F-ratio
Political interest				
How interested are you in information about what's going on in government and politics? (1–5, mean)	3.15 (151)	3.46 (70)	3.36 (70)	0.441 (p = 0.508)
Would you say that you follow what's going on in government and public affairs most of the time, some of the time, only now and then, or hardly at all? (1–4, mean)	2.42 (151)	2.90 (70)	2.79 (70)	0.643 (p = 0.424)
Internal efficacy				
Internal efficacy scale (1–5, mean)	3.04 (150)	3.29 (70)	3.28 (68)	0.007 (p = 0.932)
Given the opportunity, I feel that I could do a good job influencing public officials (1–5, mean)	3.00 (151)	3.37 (70)	3.34 (70)	0.030 (p = 0.863)
To the extent that citizens can influence politics, my efforts to do so would be more effective than the average person's (1–5, mean)	3.17 (151)	3.37 (70)	3.38 (68)	0.004 (p = 0.948)
Sometimes politics and government seem so complicated that a person like me can't really understand what's going on (1–5, mean)	2.96 (150)	3.13 (70)	3.06 (70)	0.129 (p = 0.720)
External efficacy				
External efficacy scale (1–5, mean)	2.89 (150)	3.19 (70)	2.94 (70)	2.874 (p = 0.092)
People like me don't have any say about what government does (1–5, mean)	3.22 (150)	3.63 (70)	3.39 (70)	1.89 (p = 0.172)
I don't think public officials care much what people like me think (1–5, mean)	2.56 (150)	2.74 (70)	2.49 (70)	2.036 (p = 0.156)
	(150)	(70)	(70)	

Note: All variables are coded (or have been recoded) so that higher values indicate greater levels of interest or efficacy. Only students who had completed pretests and posttests are included. Scales are additive.

the course than they did at the beginning. On every measure, as well as the additive scales, students were more interested in politics and felt more efficacious at the end of the semester than they did at the beginning.

We should, however, expect that a talented instructor who is well-trained, experienced, and committed to helping students understand government and politics would generate interest over the course of a semester. Reasonable observers might disagree about whether we would hypothesize increases in efficacy. On the one hand, when students know more, they ought to feel more empowered and efficacious. On the other hand, some of what happens in a political science course is a dispelling of myths about American government and politics, which can lead to increased cynicism and, thus, could decrease feelings of efficacy. It is clear that these students fall into the former camp, as efficacy responses were slightly higher at the end of the course as compared to the start.

Effect of Twitter Use

What remains to be determined is the extent to which there are differences in interest and efficacy at the end of the course between participants who were required to use Twitter throughout and those who were not. The last three columns in Table 4.2 compare the means for each of the target items, as well as their respective scales, separated by experimental condition. The Analysis of Variance (ANOVA) analysis reveals that none of the differences reach accepted levels of statistical significance, which means that Twitter use did not result in differences on these items. In fact, levels of interest and efficacy were slightly lower on most items among Twitter users compared to students who did not use Twitter.

Such an analysis highlights aggregate shifts in interest and efficacy. We might examine this from another perspective by looking more closely at whether individual students' changes

Table 4.3 Changes in interest and efficacy, individual-level

Difference Index (posttest—pretest)	Mean, Control (N)	Mean, treatment (N)	ANOVA F-ratio
Political interest			
How interested are you in information about what's going on in government and politics?	0.433 (60)	0.065 (62)	5.27 (p = 0.023)
Would you say that you follow what's going on in government and public affairs most of the time, some of the time, only now and then, or hardly at all?	0.433 (60)	0.387 (62)	0.104 (p = 0.748)
Internal efficacy			
Internal efficacy scale	0.483 (60)	0.833 (60)	0.826 (p = 0.365)
Given the opportunity, I feel that I could do a good job influencing public officials	0.283 (60)	0.484 (62)	1.085 (p = 0.300)
To the extent that citizens can influence politics, my efforts to do so would be more effective than the average person's	0.083 (60)	0.267 (60)	0.927 (p = 0.338)
Sometimes politics and government seem so complicated that a person like me can't really understand what's going on	0.117 (60)	0.081 (62)	0.028 (p = 0.867)
External efficacy			
External efficacy scale	0.051 (59)	0.500 (62)	1.480 (p = 0.226)
People like me don't have any say about what government does	0.119 (59)	0.371 (62)	1.189 (p = 0.278)
I don't think public officials care much what people like me think	−0.068 (59)	0.129 (62)	0.739 (p = 0.392)

Note: Difference Indexes are calculated by subtracting the score on the pretest from that of the posttest; accordingly, positive values indicate increases in interest and efficacy, respectively, while negative values represent decreases. All variables are coded (or have been recoded) so that higher values indicate greater levels of interest or efficacy. Only students who had completed pretests and posttests are included. Scales are additive.

in interest and efficacy were affected by using Twitter as a course requirement. To do so, we construct a new measure by subtracting each student's pretest response from his or her posttest response. The result is a "difference index" that runs from −4 (1 on the posttest and 5 on the pretest) to 4 (5 on the posttest and 1 on the pretest) for the efficacy items and scales as well as the second interest item. The difference index for the first interest item ("How interested are you in information about what's going on in government and politics?") runs from −3 to 3. For each of these measures, a positive sign indicates that the student's level of interest or efficacy increased over the course of the semester, while a negative sign indicates that interest or efficacy was lower at the end than at the beginning.

Results of differences in the means of these newly constructed measures appear in Table 4.3. While most of the results mirror the aggregate findings (no statistically significant difference between those who used Twitter and those who did not), the first interest item does, indeed, feature a statistically significant result. Curiously, though, it is not in the expected direction. Students who did not use Twitter had a greater increase in interest (as measured by this item) than those who did.

Discussion

The results of this experiment are sobering and present an appropriate opportunity for us to exhale and assess the potential for enhancing courses with technology with an eye toward civic education. Before acknowledging the limitations, we should be clear about the strength of the design. By asking community college students to participate, we were able to recruit a healthy pool of students who had the same course with the same professor, all within a 12-month period. Further, these students had very little experience with political science and government prior to coming into the course.

One significant potential drawback is that there might be some uniqueness to the community college students as compared to students at four-year colleges or universities. These results are not intended to be generalizable to a broader population, so it is possible that effects would be different in other contexts. Further, we need to consider the possibility of the effect of Twitter use on the instructor. That is, even though half of the students in the study were not required to use Twitter, the professor was using Twitter as part of his pedagogical strategy for students in the other course. That activity might have affected his level of engagement, ability to bring in additional material, and so on, in ways that could affect the students in the control group.

Beyond direct effects, however, students overwhelmingly indicated that they enjoyed using Twitter as a course requirement. Fifty-seven percent indicated that they strongly agreed or agreed with the statement "I enjoyed using Twitter as a requirement for this course," while only 28 percent indicated that they strongly disagreed or disagreed with that statement.[5] Further, nearly half of the participants who used Twitter as a course requirement believed that doing so increased their "interest in politics, public policy and/or political science."[6] So even if there are no direct effects apparent, there seems to be no clear downside to encouraging use of Twitter in the introductory Government course.

Conclusion

In this study, we examine the effectiveness of Twitter as a means to increase civic engagement in college students. Infusing technology into political science classrooms has the potential to help students connect in the virtual world, exchange information, and increase knowledge, all of which can contribute to increased civic engagement. With no empirical support that Twitter has an independent and positive effect on political knowledge and efficacy, it seems that while Twitter has the ability to be an effective pedagogical tool, it does not independently foster civic engagement in this context. In terms of the value of Twitter, anecdotal evidence illustrates that using it does provide an additional way to connect students to the instructor and each other while sharing knowledge, which should increase social capital. Furthermore, students enjoy it and believe that doing it increased their interest in politics.

The study of Web 2.0 technologies, and specifically Twitter, as a means to increase civic engagement is embryonic. As we move forward, we must be thoughtful about better ways to examine the effects of Twitter on indicators of civic engagement. Reassessing the rubric used to grade Twitter participation may be a way to incentivize students to use Twitter more frequently. In terms of designing future studies, while we had over 140 respondents, more than previous similar studies (Caliendo, Chod, and Muck 2013a, b), more respondents surely provides a more robust study. Moreover, all of the participants are from a community college, which presents challenges as well as benefits. Most importantly, the fact that the instructor used Twitter in some sections and not others simultaneously might have had an effect on class discussion, even in the sections where Twitter was not required. Additionally, political science majors and minors take multiple courses in which they will use Twitter; therefore, a panel study to assess whether the repeated use of Twitter translates into increased levels of civic engagement best illustrates long-term effects. While this study does not provide empirical evidence that Twitter is the answer to the long-standing question of how to engage the unengaged, there is value in pushing both pedagogically and methodologically to uncover ways to increase the political efficacy, knowledge, and interest of the Millennial generation.

Notes

1. Other studies have focused on engagement with course material, other students, and the instructor (Antenos-Conforti 2009; Borau et al. 2009; Ebner 2009; Ebner et al. 2010, Elavsky, Mislan, and Elavsky 2011; Perifanou 2009; Rinaldo, Tapp, and Laverie 2011).

2. Three-fourth of the students were enrolled in traditional face-to-face sessions, while the remaining quarter were enrolled in online sessions. Examinations reveal no correlations between delivery and key variables, so we do not differentiate in the following analysis.

3. A principal component analysis was run separately for each construct. In all three cases, only one factor was extracted. That factor accounts for 80 percent of the variance in the pretest interest items, 78 percent of the variance in the posttest interest items, 60 percent of the variance in the pretest internal efficacy items, 56 percent of the variance in the posttest internal efficacy items, 70 percent of the variance in the pretest external efficacy items, and 69 percent of the variance in the posttest external efficacy items. It is worth noting, however, that the third internal efficacy item did not load particularly powerfully in the posttest measures (0.273). Further, when we ran the procedure with all five-efficacy items, the posttest items resulted in the expected two-factor model, but the pretest items resulted in only one factor being extracted. It is possible that there was a solidification of difference between these constructs over the course of the semester.

4. Cronbach's alpha scores for the scales are as follows: internal efficacy pretest ($\alpha = 0.637$), internal efficacy posttest ($\alpha = 0.567$), external efficacy pretest ($\alpha = 0.564$), and external efficacy posttest ($\alpha = 0.544$).

5. $N = 69$.

6. $N = 69$.

References

Antenos-Conforti, Enza. 2009. "Microblogging on Twitter: Social Networking in Intermediate Italian Classes." In *The Next Generation: Social Networking and Online Collaboration in Foreign Language Learning*, edited by Lara Lomicka and Gillian Lord. San Marcos, CA: CALICO, 59–90.

Barnes, Kassandra, Raymond C. Marateo, and S. Pixy Ferris. 2007. "Teaching and Learning with the Net Generation." *Innovate* 3: 1–8.

Bartlett, Robin M. and JoNell Strough. 2003. "Multimedia versus Traditional Course Instruction in Introductory Social Psychology." *Teaching of Psychology* 30 (October): 335–338.

Beaujon, Andrew. 2012. "Half of Americans Get News Digitally, Topping Newspapers, Radio." September 27. http://www.poynter.org/latestnews/mediawire/189819/pew-tv-viewing-habit-grays-as-digital-news-consumption-tops-print-radio/ (March 1, 2013).

Bennett, Daniel and Pam Fielding. 1999. *The Net Effect: How Cyberadvocacy Is Changing the Political Landscape*. Merrifield, VA: e-advocates Press.

Bennett, Shea. 2014. "How Many Millennials, Gen Xers and Baby Boomers Use Facebook, Twitter and Instagram?" June 30. http://www.adweek.com/socialtimes/millennials-gen-x-baby-boomers-social-media/499110 (March 3, 2015).

Bimber, Bruce. 2001. "Information and Political Engagement in America: The Search for Effects of Information Technology at the Individual Level." *Political Research Quarterly* 54 (March): 53–67.

Borau, Kerstin, Carsten Ullrich, Jinjin Feng, and Ruimin Shen. 2009. "Microblogging for Language Learning: Using Twitter to Train Communicative and Cultural Competence." In *Advances in Web Based Learning—ICWL 2009*, edited by Marc Spaniol, Qing Li, Ralf Klamma, and Rynson W. H. Lau. Heidelberg: Springer, 78–87.

Browning, Graeme. 1996. *Electronic Democracy: Using the Internet to Influence Politics*. Wilton, CT: Online Inc.

Caliendo, Stephen M., Suzanne M. Chod, and William J. Muck. 2013a. "Building a Learning Community Beyond the Classroom: Using Twitter to Engage Students in Political Science." Presented at the Midwest Political Science Association annual meeting, Chicago, Illinois. http://www.mpsanet.org/Portals/0/PaperArchive/124003-Caliendo%20Chod%20Muck%20MPSA%202013.pdf (April 11, 2013).

Caliendo, Stephen M., Suzanne M. Chod, and William J. Muck. 2013b. "If We Can't Reach 'Em, Maybe Mayor @CoryBooker Can: Using Twitter to Increase Political Interest among Introduction to American Government Students." Presented at the American Political Science Association Annual Meeting, Chicago, Illinois. http://papers.ssrn.com/sol3/papers.cfm?abstract_id=2303542 (September 15, 2013).

Campbell, David E. 2008. "Voice in the Classroom: How an Open Classroom Climate Fosters Political Engagement among Adolescents." *Political Behavior* 30 (December): 437–454.

Cennamo, Katherine S., John D. Ross, and Peggy A. Ertmer. 2010. *Technology Integration for Meaningful Classroom Use: A Standards-Based Approach.* Belmont, CA: Wadsworth, Cengage Learning.

Center for Information and Research on Civic Learning and Engagement. 2015. "Civic Education." http://www.civicyouth.org/quick-facts/quick-facts-civic-education/#teachers (March 3, 2015).

Chamberlain, Adam. 2013. "The (Dis)Connection between Political Culture and External Efficacy." *American Politics Research* 41(September): 761–782.

Comber, Melissa K. 2005. "The Effects of Civic Education on Civic Skills. Fact Sheet." http://www.civicyouth.org///_05_effects_of_civic_education_on_civic_skills.pdf (March 1, 2013).

Dahlgren, Peter. 2000. "The Internet and the Democratization of Civic Culture." *Political Communication* 17 (October–December):335–340.

de Vreese, Claes H. 2007. "Digital Renaissance: Young Consumer and Citizen?" *Annals of the American Academy of Political and Social Science* 611 (May): 207–216.

Dertouzos, Michael. 1997. *What Will Be: How the New Information Marketplace Will Change Our Lives.* San Francisco: Harper.

Dori Yehudit, Judy and John Belcher. 2005. "How Does Technology-Enabled Active Learning Affect Undergraduate Students' Understanding of Electromagnetism Concepts?" *The Journal of the Learning Sciences* 14: 243–279.

Dyck, Joshua J. and Edward L. Lascher, Jr. 2009. "Direct Democracy and Political Efficacy Reconsidered." *Political Behavior* 31 (September): 401–427.

Ebner, Martin. 2009. "Interactive Lecturing by Integrating Mobile Devices and Micro-Blogging in Higher Education. *Journal of Computing and Information Technology* 17 (December) 371–381.

Ebner, Martin, Conrad Lienhardt, Matthias Rohs, and Iris Meyer. 2010. "Microblogs in Higher Education: A Chance to Facilitate Informal and Process-Oriented Learning?" *Computers & Education* 55 (August): 92–100.

Eggen, Paul D. and Don P. Kauchak. 1999. *Educational Psychology: Windows on Classrooms.* Upper Saddle River, NJ: Prentice Hall.

Elavsky, C. Michael, Cristian Mislan, and Steriani Elavsky. 2011. "When Talking Less Is More: Exploring Outcomes of Twitter Usage in the Large-Lecture Hall." *Learning, Media and Technology* 36: 215–233.

Ellison, Nicole B., Charles Steinfeld, and Cliff Lampe. 2007. "The Benefits of Facebook 'Friends': Social Capital and College Students'

Use of Online Social Network Sites." *Journal of Computer-Mediated Communication* 12 (July): 1143–1168.

Fisher, Mercedes and Derek E. Baird. 2005. "Online Learning Design That Fosters Student Support, Self-Regulation, and Retention." *Campus-Wide Information Systems* 22: 88–107.

Galston, William A. 2004. "Civic Education and Political Participation." *PS: Political Science and Politics* 2 (April): 263–266.

Gao, Fei, Tian Luo, and Ke Zhang. 2012. "Tweeting for Learning: A Critical Analysis of Research on Microblogging in Education Published in 2008–2011." *British Journal of Educational Technology* 43 (September): 783–801.

Gimpel, James G., J. Celeste Lay, and Jason E. Schuknecht. 2003. *Cultivating Democracy: Civic Environments and Political Socialization in America*. Washington, DC: Brookings Institution.

Greenhow, Christine, Beth Robelia, and Joan E. Hughes. 2009. "Learning, Teaching, and Scholarship in a Digital Age: Web 2.0 and Classroom Research: What Path Should We Take Now?" *Educational Researcher* 38 (May): 246–259.

Grossman, Lawrence K. 1995. *The Electronic Republic: Reshaping Democracy in America*. New York: Viking.

Java, Akshay, Xiaodan Song, Tim Finin, and Belle Tseng. 2007. "Why We Twitter: Understanding Microblogging Usage and Communities." In *Proceedings of the 9th WebKDD and 1st SNA-KDD 2007 Workshop on Web Mining and Social Network Analysis*. ACM, 56–65.

Jennings, M. Kent and Vicki Zeitner. 2003. "Internet Use and Civic Engagement: A Longitudinal Analysis." *Public Opinion Quarterly* 67 (November): 311–334.

Johnson, Thomas J. and Barbara E. Kaye. 1998. "A Vehicle for Engagement or a Haven for the Disaffected? Internet Use, Political Alienation, and Voter Participation." *In Engaging the Public: How Government and the Media Can Reinvigorate American Democracy*, edited by Thomas J. Johnson, Carol E. Hays, and Scott P. Hays. New York: Rowman & Littlefield, 123–135.

Jonassen, David. H. 2004. "Welcome to the Design of Constructivist Learning Environments (CLEs)." http://tiger.coe.missouri.edu/~jonassen/courses/CLE/main.html;%20http://tiger.coe.missouri.edu/~jonassen/courses/CLE/ (March 1, 2013).

Junco, Reynol, Greg Heiberger, and Eric Loken. 2011. "The Effect of Twitter on College Student Engagement and Grades." *Journal of Computer Assisted Learning* 27 (April): 119–132.

Katz, James E. and Ronald E. Rice. 2002. *Social Consequences of Internet Use: Access, Involvement, and Interaction*. Cambridge, MA: MIT Press.

Kavanaugh, Andrea. 2002. "Community Networks and Civic Engagement: A Social Network Approach: Social Networks and Computer Networks." *The Good Society* 11: 17–24.

Kwak, Haewoon, Lee Changhyun, Hosung Park, and Sue Moon. 2010. "What Is Twitter, a Social Network or a News Media?" Paper presented at the International World Wide Web (WWW) Conference, Raleigh, NC. http://an.kaist.ac.kr/~hosung/papers/2010-www-twitter.pdf (March 1, 2010).

Lane, Robert E. 1959. *Political Life: Why and How People Get Involved in Politics.* New York: Free Press.

Leighley, Jan. 1996. "Group Membership and the Mobilization of Political Participation." *Journal of Politics* 58 (May): 447–463.

Levine, Peter. 2007. *The Future of Democracy: Developing the Next Generation of American Citizens.* Lebanon, NH: University Press of New England.

Mitchell, Amy, Tom Rosenstiel, and Leah Christian. 2012. "What Facebook and Twitter Mean for News." March 19. http://www.pewresearch.org/2012/03/19/state-of-the-news-media-2012/ (March 1, 2013).

Morris, Dick. 2000. *Vote.com.* Los Angeles, CA: Renaissance Books.

Negroponte, Nicholas. 1995. *Being Digital.* New York: Knopf.

Niemi, Richard G., Stephen C. Craig, and Franco Mattei. 1991. "Measuring Political Efficacy in the 1988 National Election Study." *American Political Science Review* 85 (December): 1407–1413.

Niemi, Richard G. and Jane Junn. 1998. *Civic Education: What Makes Students Learn?* New Haven, CT: Yale University Press.

Norris, Pippa. 1999. "Who Surfs? New Technologies, Old Voters and Virtual Democracy." In *Democracy.com Governance in a Networked World*, edited by Elaine Ciulla Kamarck and Joseph S. Nye. Hollis, NH: Hollis, 45–62.

Norris, Pippa. 2001. *Digital Divide? Civic Engagement, Information Poverty and the Internet Worldwide.* Cambridge: Cambridge University Press.

Palfrey, John and Urs Gasser. 2008. *Born Digital: Understanding the First Generation of Digital Natives.* New York: Basic Books.

Perifanou, Maria A. 2009. "Language Micro-Gaming: Fun and Informal Microblogging Activities for Language Learning." *Communications in Computer and Information Science* 49: 1–14.

Pingree, Raymond J. 2011. "Effects of Unresolved Factual Disputes in the News on Epistemic Political Efficacy." *Journal of Communication* 61 (February): 22–47.

Putnam, Robert D. 1995. "Bowling Alone: America's Declining Social Capital." *Journal of Democracy* 6 (January): 65–78.

Rinaldo, Shannon B., Suzanne Tapp, and Debra A. Laverie. 2011. "Learning by Tweeting: Using Twitter as a Pedagogical Tool." *Journal of Marketing Education* 33 (August): 193–203.

Rosenstone, Stephen J. and John Mark Hansen. 1993. *Mobilization, Participation, and Democracy in America*. New York: Macmillan.

Seaman, Michael A. 1998. "Developing Visual Displays for Lecture-Based Courses." *Teaching of Psychology* 25: 141–145.

Shani, Danielle. 2012. "Measuring Political Interest." In *Improving Public Opinion Surveys: Interdisciplinary Innovation and the American National Election Studies*, edited by John H. Aldrich and Kathleen M. McGraw. Princeton, NJ: Princeton University Press, 137–157.

Smith, Aaron and Joanna Brenner. 2012. "Twitter Use 2012." May 31. http://pewinternet.org/Reports/2012/Twitter-Use-2012/Findings.aspx (March 1, 2013).

Wellman, Barry, Janet Salaff, Dimitrina Dimitrova, Laura Garton, Milena Gulia, and Caroline Haythornthwaite. 1996. "Computer Networks as Social Networks: Collaborative Work, Telework, and Virtual Community." *Annual Review of Sociology* 22 August): 213–238.

CHAPTER 5

Effectively Using Facebook to Foster Civic Engagement

Leah A. Murray

INTRODUCTION

In the early nineteenth century, Alexis de Tocqueville noted that America's democracy was one of interconnectivity, as Americans were joiners (Tocqueville 1990); what made American democracy work was people being engaged with each other in groups. This group participation has been waning for the last few decades and scholars have lamented its decline since as early as the 1980s (Coleman 1994; Galston and Levine 1998; Putnam 1993, 1995, 2000; Skocpol and Fiorina 1999). In response, higher education has worked on connecting the work students do in the community to the content learned in the classroom in an effort to reboot our participatory nature (Colby et al. 2007; Jacoby and Ehrlich 2009). As the most recent round of published Carnegie classifications indicates with its 361 competitive designations, many universities are embracing this effort in the nature of high-quality civic engagement curricula. Pedagogical research for best practices advise faculty to use the world that students live in as a textbook as they teach civic engagement (Battistoni 2002; Damon 1998; Eyler et al. 2003). Students should accomplish their civic learning in their communities as citizens, not in their classrooms.

Concomitant with this emergent research focused on strengthening American democracy, our nation entered the "connected age," which describes the "technology-assisted hyperconnectivity of learners, faculty, and institutions" (Dahlstrom, Walker, and Dziuban 2012: 6). People have quick access to much information as well as to each other. While it is doubtful that strengthening democratic institutions is their motive, it is clear that students in higher education are interested in being more connected. Students report that they would like faculty to use social networking tools more in their connection to the university community with 24 percent of students wanting their instructors to use Facebook more and 66 percent wanting more use of email (Dahlstrom, Walker, and Dziuban 2012). Students have also reported that they prefer institutions of higher education to be more engaged with social media (Tilsley 2012). According to the Pew Internet Project, 43 percent of young people aged 18–32 read blogs, 20 percent create blogs, and 67 percent use social networking sites (Jones and Fox 2009).

Given the push for civic learning coupled with students' dramatic increase in the use of technology, we need to focus our attention on the possibilities of using technology as a medium for facilitating civic engagement. Much recent research on the nexus of technology and civic engagement focuses on the Obama 2008 presidential campaign (Cogburn and Espinoza-Vasquez 2011; Fernandes et al. 2010; Vitak et al. 2011). In terms of finding political information, there was a digital divide in that election: 37 percent of people aged 18–24 accessed campaign information from social networking while only 4 percent of people aged 30–39 did the same (Kohut 2008). Other recent scholarship is mixed on whether online civic activities could result in offline behavior change with some arguing there is no difference between use of the Internet and other types of media (Baumgartner and Morris 2010; McKinney and Rill 2009) and others arguing that using technology results in more political participation such as voting, contributing to campaigns, and the like (Bimber 2003; Mossberger, Tolbert, and McNeal 2008; Shah et al. 2009; Xenos and Moy 2007). Furthermore, online political participation is less strongly linked to socioeconomic status (Smith et al. 2009). Indeed, online political participatory behavior was found to develop an individual's sense of civic skills (Ito and Bittanti 2009; Jenkins et al. 2007) and to expose an individual to contradicting political views (Wojcieszak and Mutz 2009). Also, research demonstrated that a special "get out the vote" message showing Facebook user pictures of friends generated 340,000 additional votes nationwide (Bond et al. 2012).

In contrast, digital media was also found to have no effect on the level of youth knowledge of current affairs (Bauerlein 2008) and that competence with technology plays a role in whether online tools enhance civic engagement (Campbell and Kwak 2010). Consequently, it appears that while the digital age ipso facto is no panacea for a weakening democracy, digital media can be an invaluable tool in a civically engaged classroom. For example, Bachen et al. (2008) found that online technology increased indicators of civic learning only when specific civic engagement pedagogy was deployed.

In regard to social networking specifically, 75 percent of people aged 19–29 have a profile on a social networking site as compared to 41 percent of the American population (Taylor and Keeter 2010: 1). More specifically, 86 percent of Millennials check their Facebook account every day (McCorkindale, DiStaso, and Sisco 2013: 77) and 91 percent were members of Facebook groups that they were most likely invited to join by other friends (McCorkindale, DiStaso, and Sisco 2013: 79). Mostly young people use Facebook to maintain an existing group of friends (Pempek et al. 2009) and not to make new connections but recent research has shown that the use of Facebook groups results in young people gathering information and engaging in political and civic activities (Park, Kee, and Valenzuela 2009; Woolley 2010). Other research has found that Facebook users tend to be students who are more civically engaged, so it is hard to tease out the causal relationship (Valenzuela, Park, and Kee 2009: 889). However, the more students used Facebook, the more connected they were likely to feel (Steinfield, Ellison, and Lampe 2008: 441) and generally students use Facebook to shore up offline relationships (Ellison, Steinfield, and Lampe 2007; Lampe, Ellison, and Steinfield 2007). With regard to political engagement, specifically, only Facebook groups were found to have a statistically significant positive relationship (Valenzuela, Park, and Kee 2009: 890).

Given this line of research and the possibility of enhancing civic learning with online technology and to capitalize on the unique benefits of Facebook groups, I hypothesize (H1) that a current events knowledge assignment that uses a Facebook group would create more civic engagement than a current events knowledge assignment that uses a discussion board, and (H2) that there will be more posts in the Facebook course than in the discussion board course. Students will likely become more engaged using a native technology they are comfortable and familiar with than learning management software. H1 will be supported if more posts achieve a distinguished rating on the civic engagement rubric. H2 will be supported if there are significantly more posts in the Facebook course.

METHOD

In order to see if social networking produced more civic engagement, two online Introduction to American National Government courses were examined. Each course had 50 students, all of whom were in the 18–29-year-old range. An explicit part of each course was a requirement to develop the students' current events knowledge. In one course, the discussion board feature of Canvas was used, and in another a closed group on Facebook was used. All other aspects of the courses were the same: textbook, size of class, lecture materials available, and exam expectations. The current events assignment itself was also common to both courses as the medium of the discussion was changed. However, due to the nature of the media deployed, the specificity of the assignment was different: in the Facebook course students generated current affairs awareness (Appendix 5.2) while in the discussion board course students answered questions posed by the instructor (Appendix 5.3). Secondly, this experiment allows for an unbiased test of the use of technology to increase civic engagement because the current events assignment is not specifically a civic engagement assignment. Students were not told that they would be scored on a civic engagement rubric for the assignment; they only earned credit if they submitted posts. Thus, this experiment allows us to see if participating in the Facebook environment fosters more civic engagement than participating on a discussion board because the students would create the civic engagement entirely on their own without trying to earn credit for it.

Given the literature, simply participating online in a political environment does not foster current affairs knowledge (Bauerlein 2008) but adding a pedagogical component can increase civic outcomes (Bachen et al. 2008). Therefore, in the discussion board course, students answered a discussion question on a current event (Appendix 5.3). They were required to either respond directly to the question or to another student's response. In the Facebook course, students were required to (1) create civic events and invite their peers to them; (2) post links to *New York Times'* political stories and provide reasoning in the comments section; (3) comment on other students' posts of New York Times stories; and (4) upload media to Facebook from some civic event they attended (Appendix 5.2). All of these interactions in both courses occurred strictly in an online environment, which helps control for instructor influence as neither set of students ever met with an instructor. The only difference was the Facebook course deployed social media while the discussion board course deployed a more traditional online-learning method of interaction.

Every Facebook post and discussion board post was measured on a civic engagement rubric created for Weber State University and that is used campus wide for assessing civic engagement (Appendix 5.1). This rubric has four learning outcomes: (1) civic knowledge: applying discipline specific knowledge to civic engagement; (2) civic skills: engaging in a process to solve and increase awareness of some civic problem; (3) civic values: having a disposition to the world that understands the need for civic engagement; and (4) civic action: demonstrating continued commitment to engaged citizenship. Each learning outcome has four levels of understanding: (1) novice, which entails the student simply identifying knowledge or activities; (2) apprentice, which entails the student explaining with a bit more detail the knowledge or activities that pertain to the civic work; (3) proficient, which entails the student articulating an understanding of broader systemic forces at work; and (4) distinguished, which entails the student creating civic engagement him or herself. Each post was coded on the learning outcome as well as the level of understanding. If a post represented more than one learning outcome, it was coded twice, once for each outcome. A student researcher coded the posts as well, with names removed, and we worked to achieve an interrater reliability at 0.81.

Findings

Of the 539 posts in the two courses, the lion's share was on the Facebook assignment at 75.1 percent (Table 5.1). Thus, there is evidence to support H2. The familiarity that students have using social networking tools (Kohut 2008; Jones and Fox 2009) created an environment in which they felt more

Table 5.1 Posts on assignments

Variable label	Frequency	Percent
Discussion posts	134	24.9
Facebook posts	405	75.1
Total	539	100

Source: Data collected from assignments in class.

comfortable engaging in political conversation. Given that students were more comfortable, their productivity was three times higher. Adding the pedagogical expectation of current affairs awareness to the use of Facebook did result in more discipline-specific knowledge; 77.9 percent of the posts demonstrated knowledge that political science connects to current affairs (Table 5.2). The other benefit of this abundant creation of current affairs knowledge is that students develop a peripheral awareness of current events. At least one student posted a *New York Times* story on the class's Facebook group covering almost every major current event in the semester. The Facebook assignment thus created a virtual water cooler at which they "discussed" political events. In one way, this addresses the issue of increasing media choice of students by putting them in a situation in which they are made aware of political news (Prior 2005). Again, because the Facebook assignment happened in the students' more natural habitat than the discussion board, they were more likely to participate, and in turn, this more frequent participation translated into more political event awareness.

Each of the 539 posts was coded on two dimensions, first on which learning outcome the post met (Table 5.2) and second on which level of depth the student reached with regard to the learning outcome (Table 5.3). Not surprisingly, the vast majority of students posted events that related to discipline-specific knowledge as they were connecting the material to what they learned in the class. This is intuitive because it tracks what

Table 5.2 Current events outcome in percentages

Variable label	Frequency	Percent
Civic knowledge	420	77.9
Civic skills	38	7.1
Civic values	81	15
Total	539	100

Source: Data collected from assignments in class.

Table 5.3 Current events rating on rubric

Variable label	Frequency	Percent
No rating	54	10
Novice	225	41.7
Apprentice	163	30.2
Proficient	89	16.5
Distinguished	8	1.5
Total	539	99.9

Source: Data collected from assignments in class, percentage not equaling 100 is due to rounding.

students generally would be expected to learn in an introductory course. Given that the civic knowledge learning outcome is about applying discipline-specific knowledge, we would expect new students to the material to focus on the content and connecting said content to the current events. The assignment did not ask students to learn a specific civic engagement outcome, but the whole course was about learning the discipline. Therefore, we would expect students to generate this learning outcome the most.

Each post was also coded on the level of learning achieved, and again, intuitively, most of the civic engagement happened at the novice level. Students in an introductory-level course are generally at the stage of identifying concepts rather than being able to explain connections, much less creating new knowledge.

One interesting point about using Facebook in a classroom assignment that relates to the comfort level students have using social networking is demonstrated in Table 5.4. Students were willing to "talk" to each other using comments. The bulk of the discussion about current events happened in comments back and forth among students. They were much more likely to discuss politics in this venue than they were in the online discussion forum. Students are more attuned to this mode of conversation; they are used to commenting on "friends" posts on Facebook. Another interesting finding here is that 3.9 percent of posts were not assigned. All of these not-assigned posts were submitted in the Facebook course. This is an indicator of how the medium made the content more appealing to students, thus sparking more independent posting.

In contrast, the nature of the discourse in the discussion board course created a one-to-one phenomenon in which students simply answered the questions. Furthermore, as one can see in Table 5.4, by the time students were answering Discussions 4, 5, and 6, the numbers dropped off as they were less interested in the conversation. This finding is particularly interesting because one might think that the conversation would increase as students became more familiar with the content and the medium

Table 5.4 Types of posts

Variable label	Frequency	Percent
Discussion 1	25	4.6
Discussion 2	27	5
Discussion 3	27	5
Discussion 4	16	3
Discussion 5	16	3
Discussion 6	23	4.3
New York times story	55	10.2
Comment	299	55.5
Media upload	13	2.4
Event invitation	17	3.2
Not assigned post	21	3.9
Total	539	100.1

Source: Data collected from assignments in class, percentage not equaling 100 is due to rounding.

of the discussion board. Yet, it appears that a discussion board used exclusively for the class grew more tedious over the course of the semester. On the Facebook assignment, however, students were generating their own conversations. The numbers of comments indicate that they were talking around their "virtual" water cooler on their own volition rather than a desire to simply meet some course requirements.

Clearly the Facebook assignment is superior to a traditional discussion board in generating volume of current events conversation. More importantly, however, there is some evidence to support H1 in that the Facebook assignment generated more civic engagement than the traditional discussion board. The traditional discussion board only generated conversations about civic knowledge, for which students applied discipline-specific knowledge to civic engagement. All these discussion posts demonstrated only one learning outcome. On the other hand, the Facebook assignment dispersed across three learning outcomes. To be fair, the bulk of the conversation stream was in the civic knowledge outcome, but as we see in Table 5.5, 9.4 percent of the posts demonstrated civic skills and a full 20 percent demonstrated civic values.

However, while more civic learning was triggered in the Facebook course, it was not the case that the work was necessarily at a higher level of learning. In Table 5.6, we see that while there were more outcomes demonstrated, the discussion

Table 5.5 Learning outcome by assignment type

Outcome	Discussion	Facebook	Total
Civic knowledge	100	70.6	420
Civic skills	0	9.4	38
Civic values	0	20	81
Total	100	100	539
N	134	405	539
			X^2*

*$p < 0.000$.
Source: Data collected from assignments in class.

Table 5.6 Civic engagement rating by overall assignment type

Rating	Discussion	Facebook	Total
No rating	11.2	9.6	54
Novice	36.6	43.5	225
Apprentice	32.1	29.6	163
Proficient	20.1	15.3	89
Distinguished	0	2.0	8
Total	100	100	539
N	134	405	539
			X^2

Source: Data collected from assignments in class.

board assignment did have higher percentages of the mid-range ratings at apprentice and proficient. The one distinction to note is that while there were zero distinguished level posts in the discussion board assignment, 2 percent of the Facebook posts rose to the highest level of creating knowledge. Perhaps the reason we are not seeing a significant difference in ratings by assignment type is the high volume of comment chatter in the Facebook assignment.

While this is good for H2, the Facebook course would create more participation, it may be causing a problem for H1; the Facebook course would create a higher level of learning in civic engagement because quite a bit of that conversation was at a low level of learning.

Tables 5.7 and 5.8 demonstrate that while there was not a significant difference in civic engagement by the overall course assignment, there are significant differences when we look at the specific type of post. Table 5.8 demonstrates that students using Facebook explained their civic engagement well when they were posting stories from the *New York Times*, but not so when they were creating invitations to political events for students. Also, 100 percent of the events were civic skills-oriented as they were mobilizing students to attend events, but all these were at the novice level as none of them offered any explanation

Table 5.7 Civic engagement rating by post for discussion

Rating	1	2	3	4	5	6	Total
No rating	12	11.1	7.4	18.5	63	11.1	15
Novice	60	37	18.5	25	43.8	34.8	49
Apprentice	12	14.8	63	56.2	43.8	12.5	43
Proficient	16	37	11.1	12.5	12.5	26.1	27
Distinguished	0	0	0	0	0	0	0
Total	100	100	100	100	100	100	
N							134
							X^2*

*$p < 0.000$.
Source: Data collected from assignments in class.

Table 5.8 Civic engagement rating by post for Facebook

Rating	NYT post	Comment	Media	Event	Not assigned	Total
No rating	1.8	11.7	7.7	0	9.5	39
Novice	25.5	43.5	38.5	100	47.6	176
Apprentice	43.6	30.1	23.1	0	14.3	120
Proficient	29.1	13.7	7.7	0	19	62
Distinguished	0	1	23.1	0	9.5	8
Total	100	100	100	100	100	
N						405
						X^2*

*$p < 0.000$.
Source: Data collected from assignments in class.

for why they invited other students. Another notable item demonstrated in Table 5.7 is that in the discussion posts assignment students improved over the course of the semester. The novice rating decreased while the apprentice rating increased. As Discussion 1 was early in the semester and Discussion 6 was late, this would suggest a learning curve in civic engagement more generally. As the Facebook assignment did not require students to do their four submissions in any specific order, we cannot make any claims about a learning curve. The best rating for individual submissions was the media upload because students were creating knowledge when they commented explaining why they chose that item to upload. When asked to do this, students generally did a better job with regard to their civic engagement. Thus, in the Facebook course, requiring students to explain why they were posting resulted in higher levels of learning. Both the sharing of a *New York Times* article and the uploading of a media item included an explanation and both types of posts had higher levels of learning. Thus, connecting the pedagogical purpose to the social media does result in a deeper level of civic engagement.

CONCLUSION

The type of assignment matters for fostering civic engagement: if social media is deployed, students will participate more; if an explanation of why the student is choosing to share is required, the students will demonstrate higher civic engagement. Even when not required, the Facebook course generated substantially more chatter about politics. A number of students posted pictures of themselves voting or registering to vote, and as Bond et al. (2012) note, this may have mobilized other students to vote as well.

My expectation was that the Facebook course would generate more civic engagement and there is some evidence to support this. Posts in the Facebook course were dispersed across more civic learning outcomes than in the discussion board course, in which students focused on applying discipline specific knowledge to current affairs. However, posts in the Facebook course were not necessarily at a higher level of learning. One caveat is that the Facebook course did generate deeper civic engagement when the post required an explanation, thus demonstrating the importance of applying pedagogical standards to the online setting (Bachen et al. 2008).

Secondly, I expected that due to the comfort level of Millennials in the social media environment, there would be quite a bit more conversation in the Facebook course. There is evidence to support this as students produced three times as many posts in the Facebook course as they did in the discussion board course. The power of the pedagogical facet of Facebook peripheral awareness should be explored more as it adds to both civic engagement and political event knowledge. Perhaps the collective knowledge the class can generate without too much effort on any one individual student's part makes all students more knowledgeable on political current events.

Appendix 5.1 Rubric

Civic Knowledge involves the process of applying discipline specific knowledge to civic engagement. Artifacts for this area demonstrate the student's ability to apply facts and theories from areas of academic study to civic engagement including their own participation in civic life, politics, and government.

Novice

- Identifies knowledge (facts, theories, etc.) from one's own academic study/field/discipline that is relevant to civic engagement.
- Identifies knowledge from one's own participation in civic life, politics, and government that is relevant to civic engagement.

Apprentice

- Explains knowledge (facts, theories, etc.) from one's own academic study/field/discipline to civic engagement.
- Explains knowledge from one's own participation in civic life, politics, and government that is relevant to civic engagement.

Proficient

- Articulates systemic causes for social issues using knowledge from one's own academic study/field/discipline to civic engagement and from one's own participation in civic life, politics, and government.

Distinguished

- Creates new meaning from one's own academic study/field/discipline about one's own participation in civic life, politics, and government.
- *Civic Skills* involves the demonstration of engaging in a process to solve and increase the awareness of some civic problem. Artifacts for this area demonstrate the student's ability to collaboratively work across and within community contexts and structures.

Novice

- Identifies activities that positively impact the greater good with little or no mention of involvement in the community to address a civic problem.

Apprentice

- Explains how one's occasional involvement in the community addresses a civic problem.
- Explains how one took individual action to address the problem.

Proficient

- Articulates how one's frequent involvement in the community through direct service or advocacy efforts addresses a civic problem.
- Articulates one's ability to recruit others to effect change and use effective communication skills to increase civic awareness of a problem.

Distinguished

- Creates sustainable involvement over time through direct service, projects, or advocacy efforts.
- Creates space in the community to systemically address underlying causes, not only surface symptoms, of a civic problem.
Creates new ideas and becomes a catalyst for change.
- *Civic Values* involves having a disposition to the world that understands the need for civic engagement. Artifacts for this area

demonstrate the student's sense of efficacy as well as respect for diversity, justice, and equity.

Novice

- Identifies a disposition to the world that advocates addressing civic problems when asked to do so by an external source or authority with limited evidence of personal investment in solving civic problems.

Apprentice

- Explains how one's disposition advocates people taking social responsibility and civic engagement upon themselves to address a civic problem.
- Explains that one wants to make a difference without elaborating on the complexities of what it takes to do so.
- Proficient
- Articulates one's personal values to make a difference in society and elaborates on the complexities of what it takes to do so.
- Articulates the need for examining the role of established systems and structures that reproduce patterns of injustice over time.
- Distinguished
- Creates a personal ethic that clearly aligns with civic actions and endorses the responsibilities of an active citizen in society.
- Creates an optimistic yet realistic assessment of the personal impact one can have on civic problems and demonstrates a disposition to question and change established systems.
- *Civic Action* involves continued commitment to engaged citizenship. The artifact for this area is a capstone that demonstrates the student's competency.

Novice

- Identify one's commitment to current civic engagement experience but demonstrates no clear commitment to future action.
- Apprentice
- Explains one's commitment to civic engagement experiences now and in the future without a clear plan for how that action would come to fruition.

Proficient

- Articulates a clear plan for future civic engagement and demonstrates a commitment to service that is derived from personal experience and a desire to continue.

Distinguished

- Creates a clear plan for civic engagement having taken the initial steps in the implementation of this plan, for example an intentional choice of a major or career path to improve society or to serve others.
- Creates a connection between one's personal knowledge and skills and addressing civic problems.
- Creates an understanding of education as a privilege/opportunity that places an added responsibility to act on behalf of others.

Appendix 5.2: Facebook Assignment

CURRENT EVENTS

In order to teach you how to become fluent in conversations about current political events, we will use a class Facebook page. You will be required to interact on Facebook at least four times, although you can certainly do so more often. You need to use Facebook with as much privacy as you desire. Make sure to either create a new identity for yourself or to set your settings at high levels of privacy if you are concerned.

These are due periodically throughout the semester. You must submit that you posted on Facebook on Canvas or I will not grade it. You can submit a screen capture or submit what you posted. You can do them all early, but you have to have one complete by each date. You also *cannot* repeat another student's post. For example, if some other person posts that there is an inauguration before you get to it, you have to find something else.

The required interactions are as follows:

1. You will create a political event and invite the members of the page to the event. You do not have to organize the event, although it could be an event you organize, you just have to create a Facebook event for something political that is happening. This event has to be taking place, but can be taking place anywhere: in your hometown, on campus, anywhere.
2. You will upload a media item to the page that demonstrates you attended some political event or was witness to some political event. Again, this could be the same as the event you created or

it could be something different. It could also be something you saw and caught using a camera.

    a. If you have issues figuring out how to do this piece, please let me know and I will help you.

3. You will create a link on the page to a New York Times political story. In the comments section you will explain why the story interested you and what you think the implications are of that news item.

4. You will comment on another student's New York Times link reacting to the story and to some student's comment. Your reaction can be to any student who commented, it does not have to be to the original student posting. But it must be *civil*.

Appendix 5.3: Discussion Assignment

Discussion 1 question:

In this election cycle, Super Political Action Committees have gotten quite a bit of coverage. Comment on the effect of Super PACs on American elections.

Discussion 2 question:

Last week, New York City's mayor asked for a ban on drinks larger than 16oz. This week, California voters are considering putting a $1 tax on cigarettes. What are the reasons for governments adding taxes or trying to limit unhealthy habits? Is it a good or bad idea?

Discussion 3 question:

The past couple of weeks candidate Mitt Romney has been trying out different vice-presidential nominee possibilities. Choose who you think would be the best vice-presidential nominee for Romney and explain why.

Discussion 4 question:

This past week the Supreme Court handed down a number of decisions. Choose one that you think is very important— explain why it is important and what you think about what they decided.

Discussion 5 question:

There are quite a few issues being bantered between presidential candidates Obama and Romney. Choose one, identify the different stances and what you think about their positions.

Discussion 6 question:

Choose any current event that happened this summer that you found the most interesting. Explain why you found it to be the most interesting and discuss its implications.

References

Bachen, Christine et al. 2008. "Civic Engagement, Pedagogy, and Information Technology on Web Sites for Youth." *Political Communication* 25: 290–310.

Battistoni, Richard. 2002. "What Is Good Citizenship." In *Civic Engagement Across the Curriculum*, edited by Richard Battistoni. Providence: Campus Compact.

Bauerlein, Mark. 2008. *The Dumbest Generation: How the Digital Age Stupefies Young Americans and Jeopardizes Our Future*. New York: Jeremy P. Tarcher/Penguin.

Baumgartner, Jody C. and Jonathan S. Morris. 2010. "MyFaceTube Politics: Social Networking Web Sites and Political Engagement of Young Adults." *Social Science Computer Review* 28: 28–44.

Bimber, Bruce. 2003. *Information and American Democracy*. Cambridge: Cambridge University Press.

Bond, Robert M. et al. 2012. "A 61-Million-Person Experiment in Social Influence and Political Mobilization." *Nature* 489: 295–298.

Campbell, Scott W. and Nojin Kwak. 2010. "Mobile Communication and Civic Life: Linking Patterns of Use to Civic and Political Engagement." *Journal of Communication* 60: 536–555.

Cogburn, D. L. and Fatima K. Espinoza-Vasquez. 2011. "From Networked Nominee to Networked Nation: Examining the Impact of Web 2.0 and Social Media on Political Participation and Civic Engagement in the 2008 Obama Campaign." *Journal of Political Marketing* 10: 189–213.

Colby, Anne, Thomas Ehrlich, Elizabeth Beaumont, and Josh Corngold. 2007. *Educating for Democracy: Preparing Undergraduates for Responsible Political Engagement*, 1st ed. San Francisco: John Wiley & Sons.

Coleman, James. 1994. *Foundations of Social Theory*. Cambridge, MA: Harvard University Press.

Dahlstrom, Eden, J. D. Walker, and Charles Dziuban. 2013. *ECAR Study of Undergraduate Students and Information Technology*. EDUCAUSE Center for Analysis and Research.

Damon, William. 1998. "The Path to Civil Society Goes Through the University." *Chronicle of Higher Education* 16 (October): B3–B5.

de Tocqueville, Alexis. 1990. *Democracy in America*, edited by Phillips Bradley. New York: Knopf Doubleday.

Ellison, Nicole, Charles Steinfeld, and Cliff Lampe. 2007. The Benefits of Facebook 'Friends': Exploring the Relationship Between College Students' Use of Online Social Networks and Social Capital." *Journal of Computer-Mediated Communication* 12: 1143–1168.

Eyler, Janet S., Dwight E. Giles, Christine M. Stenson, and Charlene J. Gray. 2003. "At a Glance: What We Know About the Effects of Service-Learning on College Students, Faculty, Institutions, and Communities, 1993–2000, 3rd ed." In *Introduction to Service-Learning Toolkit*, 2nd ed, edited by Campus Compact. Providence: Campus Compact.

Fernandes, Juliana, Magda Giurcanu, Kevin W. Bowers, and Jeffrey C. Neely. 2010. "The Writing on the Wall: A Content Analysis of College Students' Facebook Groups for the 2008 Presidential Election." *Mass Communication and Society* 13 (5): 653–675.

Galston, William A. and Peter Levine. 1998. "America's Civic Condition: A Glance at the Evidence." In *Community Works: The Revival of Civil Society in America*, edited by E. J. Dionne Jr. Washington, DC: Brookings Institution Press.

Ito, Mizuko and Matteo Bittanti. 2009. *Hanging Out, Messing Around and Geeking Out: Living and Learning with New Media*. Cambridge, MA: MIT Press.

Jacoby, Barbara and Thomas Ehrlich. 2009. *Civic Engagement in Higher Education: Concepts and Practices*. San Francisco: John Wiley & Sons.

Jenkins, Henry et al. 2007. *Confronting the Challenges of Participatory Culture: Media Education for the 21st Century*. Cambridge, MA: MIT Press.

Jones, Sydney and Susannah Fox. 2009. *Pew Internet Project Data Memo*. Washington, DC: Pew Internet and American Life Project. Available at http://www.pewinternet.org/~/media//Files/Reports/2009/PIP_Generations_2009.pdf.

Kohut, Andrew. 2008. *Social Networking and Online Videos Take Off: Internet's Broader Role in Campaign, 2008*. Washington, DC: Pew Research Center for the People and the Press. Available at http://www.people-press.org/2008/01/11/internets-broader-role-in-campaign-2008/.

Lampe, Cliff, Nicole B. Ellison, and Charles Steinfeld. 2007. "A Familiar Face(book): Profile Elements as Signals in an Online Social Network." Proceedings of Conference on Human Factors in Computing Systems. New York: ACM Press.

McCorkindale, Tina, Marcia W. DiStaso, and Hilary Fussell Sisco. 2013. "How Millennials are Engaging and Building Relationships with Organizations on Facebook." The Journal of Social Media in Society 2 (1): 66–87.

McKinney, Mitchell S. and Leslie A. Rill. 2009. "Not Your Parents' Presidential Debates: Examining the Effects of the CNN? YouTube Debates on Young Citizens' Civic Engagement." Communication Studies 60 (4): 392–406.

Mossberger, Karen, Caroline J. Tolbert, and Ramona S. McNeal. 2008. Digital Citizenship. Cambridge, MA: MIT Press.

Park, Namsu, Kerk F. Kee, and Sebastian Valenzuela. 2009. "Being Immersed in Social Networking Environment: Facebook Groups, Uses and Gratifications, and Social Outcomes." CyberPsychology & Behaviors 12 (6): 729–733.

Pempek, Tiffany A., Yevdokiya A. Yermolayeva, and Sandra L. Calvert. 2009. "College Students' Social Networking Experiences on Facebook." Journal of Applied Developmental Psychology 30: 227–238.

Prior, Markus. 2005. "New vs. Entertainment: How Increasing Media Choice Widens Gaps in Political Knowledge and Turnout." American Journal of Political Science 49 (3): 577–592.

Putnam, Robert D. 1993. Making Democracy Work: Civic Traditions in Modern Italy. Princeton, NJ: Princeton University Press.

Putnam, Robert D. 1995. "Bowling Alone: America's Declining Social Capital." Journal of Democracy 6:1: 65–78.

Putnam, Robert D. 2000. Bowling Alone: Civic Disengagement in America. New York: Simon and Schuster.

Shah, Dhavan V., Jack M. McLeod, and Nam-jin Lee. 2009. "Communication Competence as a Foundation for Civic Competence: Processes of Socialization into Citizenship." Political Communication 26: 102–117.

Skocpol, Theda. 1999. "Advocates without Members: the Recent Transformation of American Civic Life." In Civic Engagement in American Democracy, edited by Theda Skocpol and Morris P. Fiorina. Washington, DC: Brookings Institution Press.

Skocpol, Theda, and Morris P. Fiorina. 1999. Civic Engagement in American Democracy. Washington, DC: Brookings Institution

Smith, Aaron, Kay Lehman Schlozman, Sidney Verba, and Henry Brady. 2009. The Internet and Civic Engagement. Washington, DC: Pew

Internet and American Life Project. Available at http://www.pewinternet.org/~/media//Files/Reports/2009/The%20Internet%20 and%20Civic%20Engagement.pdf.

Steinfield, Charles, Nicole B. Ellison, and Cliff Lampe. 2008. "Social Capital, Self-Esteem, and Use of Online Social Network Sites: A Longitudinal Analysis." *Journal of Applied Developmental Psychology* 29: 434–445.

Taylor, Paul and Scott Keeter. 2010. "Millennials: Confident. Connected. Open to Change." *Millennials.* Washington, DC: Pew Internet and American Life Project. Available at http://www.pewsocialtrends.org/ files/2010/10/millennials-confident-connected-open-to-change.pdf.

Tilsley, Alexandra. 2012. "Social Networks and College Choices." *Insider Higher Ed.* Available at www.insidehighered.com/ news/2012/09/24/survey-examines-how-prospective-students-use-social-media-research-colleges#ixzz27W9CuPYr.

Valenzuela, Sebastian, Namsu Park, and Kerk F. Kee. 2009. "Is There Social Capital in a Social Network Site?: Facebook Use and College Students' Life Satisfaction, Trust, and Particpation." *Journal of Computer-Mediated Communication* 14 (4): 875–901.

Vitak, Jessica, Paul Zube, Andrew Smock, Caleb T. Carr, Nicole Ellison, and Cliff Lampe. 2011. "It's Complicated: Facebook Users' Political Participation in the 2008 Election." *Cyberpsychology, Behavior, and Social Networking* 14 (3): 107–114.

Wojcieszak, Magdalena E. and Diana C. Mutz. 2009. "Online Groups and Political Discourse: Do Online Discussion Spaces Facilitate Exposure to Political Disagreement?" *Journal of Communication* 59: 40–56.

Woolley, Julia K. 2010. "The 2008 Presidential Election, 2.0: A Content Analysis of User-Generated Political Facebook Groups." *Mass Communication & Society* 13 (5): 631–652.

Xenos, Michael and Patricia Moy. 2007. "Direct and Differential Effects of the Internet on Political and Civic Engagement." *Journal of Communication* 57: 704–718.

Conclusion

Suzanne M. Chod and William J. Muck

This book stands as part of a broader effort to think creatively about how to best use the college classroom to develop the civic health of our democracy. A consensus has emerged within political science that instructors have an important role to play in engaging the civically unengaged, and in particular the Millennial generation. While there has been extensive research on the topic of civic and political engagement, the chapters in this volume address what we believe to be an important gap in that literature. Specifically, we argue that field has failed to fully explore whether the use of Web 2.0 technologies in the classroom has any role to play in fostering civic engagement. The authors offer both empirical and theoretical explorations of the ways in which technology might help the Millennial generation feel civically connected.

The studies, a number of which are the first of their kind, help push forward the conversation about promoting civic engagement. They ask whether breaking down the walls of the traditional classroom might enable a better connection between students and their government. The findings also reinforce the importance of bringing a scientific approach to discussions of civic engagement. It would be easy to assume simply that because this generation of students is so deeply connected with technology that its use in a political science classroom will automatically translate into increased levels of civic engagement. Yet as the chapters in this book demonstrate, this is not necessarily the case. There is much work yet to be done, and it is vital that we continue to explore—using scholarly methods—how the well-designed use of technology in the classroom can enable civic interest and engagement.

As a whole, the chapters from this edition reveal the variety of ways that technology can be used to supplement the traditional classroom. The range of approaches suggests that there is no one "right" way to incorporate technology into the classroom. The contributors review the use of high-profile social media sites (Facebook and Twitter), online classes, as well as more informal online activities. It is clear that instructors now have a host of technological options in their pedagogical toolbox.

The connections between the chapters are significant and worthy of a few moments of reflection. One major takeaway point is that these virtual communities help students develop a sense that they are also part of an important political community. The use of Web 2.0 technology in the college classroom creates an "always open" learning space where students can engage politics in their own time and way. The Shulman chapter reminds us of the importance of how messages are conveyed to students. Using accessible language and creating a supportive normative environment for students will increase their confidence in expressing and exploring their political views. This finding is reinforced by Caliendo, Chod, Muck, and Schreck's look at Twitter and Murray's examination of Facebook. Each study reports students' enjoyment using social media in the classroom, which is not surprising given how frequently students use Facebook and Twitter for their personal interactions. Over time one would expect this activity to translate into increased levels of civic interest and engagement, but further study is needed before such a conclusion can be reached. Moffett and Rice do find a strong connection between online political expression and more traditional forms of offline civic engagement. Students who use social media to connect with candidates or political parties are significantly more likely to contact government officials or newspapers. In other words, meaningful online political activity can translate into offline political engagement, at least in the short term.

A second important connection across the chapters is the potential for Web 2.0 technologies to increase the overall frequency of student interaction with and discussion of politics. Here we are talking about increased communication between students as well as between students and their instructors. Putnam (1993) and others have found that increasing the frequency of social interaction helps build social capital. That is to say, regular social interaction helps develop the networks of civic engagement that sustain long-term cooperation and norms of reciprocity. The formal classroom can be an intimidating environment for some students and, as a result, curb participation. By contrast, online activities provide students with a less intimidating and more comfortable environment to share their political views. Virtual communities also offer students additional time to think and reflect upon the ideas and concepts introduced in the formal classroom.

Shulman finds that the frequency of political communication has a direct impact on levels of political participation of young people. Her calls for intervention strategies that create more opportunities for political communication connect well with the other chapters in the book. For instance, Murray notes that students frequently used Facebook even when not required, and that it generated significantly higher levels of political chatter. Whether it is Facebook, Twitter, or online discussion boards, students have an instantaneous way to connect and share information with the instructor and their fellow students. While the studies on Facebook and Twitter produce mixed results on the question of promoting civic engagement, it may simply be that using these mechanisms for one semester is too short of a duration to generate measurable improvement. The fact that Corbin and Wisecup's examination of entirely online classes finds no significant difference between online and face-to-face classes in generating civic engagement is encouraging.

The research in this book also raises questions for the broader social capital literature, where scholars are just beginning to grapple with the impact that social media has on the development of social capital. It is not yet clear whether Facebook and Twitter will be a positive or negative force for social capital; those findings will inevitably have implications for the civic engagement literature. For example, we must consider whether the ability of Facebook and/or Twitter to help generate social capital in society at large will result in (or, perhaps, be driven by) civic engagement in and from the classroom?

Because the results presented in the chapters of this collection do not illustrate that technology is the magic wand needed to engage the unengaged, we must consider what pedagogical, theoretical, and empirical adjustments can be made. First, when choosing a particular technology in the classroom, the instructor must have a purpose and objective in mind. What will using Twitter, Facebook, or an online discussion board achieve that not using it cannot? Additionally, and more likely, how can including technology in the classroom highlight or play upon existing tendencies and interests of students? This is where following Jonassen's recommendations for online courses, as discussed in the Caliendo, Chod, Muck, and Schreck chapter, are useful. If instructors are aware of students' existing online presence, as well as the likelihood that those who take political science courses already have a heightened sense of political efficacy and interest, choosing the right technology will help increase civic engagement both anecdotally and empirically.

In terms of theoretical contributions, these chapters represent a rich and novel infusing of pedagogy, technology, communications, and political science literatures. To fully understand the impact of technology on civic engagement, it is imperative to examine all angles. It is not enough to draw on political science literature and use it as the foundation for both pedagogical choices as well as empirical work without considering the literature on and theoretical contributions of the scholarship of teaching. Drawing upon this literature is consistent with work on traditional classroom mechanisms to increase civic engagement (see Campbell 2008; Hibbing and Theiss-Morse 1996), so it is imperative to do the same for work on nontraditional ways, such as infusing technology. Therefore, we need to lean on the technology literature to instruct us on what each method can provide our students and how it may or may not achieve certain objectives. Moreover, Shulman notes, the way politics is communicated, especially within and across groups, provides a more nuanced way to examine instructional approaches to increasing civic engagement in college students. Overall, the weaving of multidisciplinary literatures and theories in the chapters of this collection illustrate the complex nature of our responsibility to reach the Millennials; it serves as a call to researchers to continue to do the same when examining this further.

The pedagogical and theoretical contributions of the works in this volume are the first of their kind, and more importantly, a critical step in advancing a limited understanding of the dynamics explored in existing studies. Nonetheless, most of the improvement to the existing studies, both in this collection and elsewhere, must be empirical. With small samples, experimental and quasi-experimental limitations, and difficulty disentangling all of the factors that lead to increased interest, efficacy, and overall civic engagement, much more work must be done. The authors of all chapters employ rigorous methodologies, as opposed to (and sometimes in addition to) anecdotal evidence or observation, to attempt to provide evidence to support expectations. Even so, issues such as self-selection and small sample sizes need to be addressed in future studies. Further, these studies, due to their novelty, are all limited in terms of failure to capture persistence. Future work must employ time-series and panel designs to determine whether any increased efficacy, interest, or engagement is "sticky." To find increases in these constructs during the time when a student is enrolled in a course is important, but if there is no value added over the long term, we must resist over-interpreting the effects.

Both the impetus for and contribution of this book are the same; uncovering the ways in which introducing technology into the college classroom may increase civic engagement. The lack of existing research answering this question called for these questions to be addressed directly. The studies contained herein offer a beginning to that timely conversation. While this work marks a notable start, more work needs to be done specifically regarding the incorporation of technology, as well as more generally the importance of how we communicate with our students about politics. We call upon teacher-scholars who are committed to the integration and study of ways to engage the unengaged to make informed pedagogical choices, execute empirical studies, and help expand this emerging field of study in political science.

References

Campbell, David E. 2008. "Voice in the Classroom: How an Open Classroom Climate Fosters Political Engagement among Adolescents." *Political Behavior* 30 (December): 437–454.

Hibbing, John R. and Elizabeth Theiss-Morse. 1996. "Civics is Not Enough: Teaching Barbarics in K-12." *PS: Political Science and Politics* 29 (March): 57–62.

Putnam, Robert. 1993. *Making Democracy Work: Civic Traditions in Modern Italy*. Princeton, NJ: Princeton University Press.

List of Contributors

Stephen M. Caliendo is Professor of Political Science at North Central College. His research focuses on political psychology and political communication. He is the author of *Inequality in America: Race, Poverty, and Fulfilling Democracy's Promise* and co-author of *Race Appeal: How Candidates Invoke Race in U.S. Political Campaigns*.

Suzanne M. Chod is an assistant professor of political science at North Central College. Her commitment to helping students become more active and engaged citizens led to a research agenda that empirically examines how pedagogical choices can contribute to increasing political efficacy and interest in Millennials.

Tanya Buhler Corbin is an assistant professor at Radford University. She holds a doctorate in political science and Masters in public policy from Claremont Graduate University. Her primary area of research focuses on the politics and policy changes after crises and disasters and their interrelationship with traditionally marginalized groups. Other research areas of interest include the scholarship of teaching and learning, and congressional policymaking.

Kenneth W. Moffett is Associate Professor of Political Science at Southern Illinois University Edwardsville. His areas of research include Congress and the Presidency as well as civic activity among youth voters. His work in these areas has been published in, or is forthcoming at *Legislative Studies Quarterly, American Politics Research, Congress and the Presidency, Social Science Quarterly, Party Politics, and Social Science Computer Review*.

William J. Muck is Associate Professor of Political Science and Coordinator of the Global Studies program at North Central College. His research interest are in the fields of international peace and security, transitional justice, and the practice of overt and covert military intervention. His most current work explores the funding patterns of global transitional justice institutions.

Leah A. Murray is an associate professor in the Department of Political Science and Philosophy at Weber State University. Her primary research interests are in American politics: the presidency, Congress, elections, and youth and politics. She received a Bachelor of Arts in political science and also in newspaper journalism from Syracuse University in 1996 and her Doctor of Philosophy in political science from the University of Albany in 2004.

Laurie L. Rice is an associate professor of political science at Southern Illinois Edwardsville and coordinator of the Civic Education Project @SIUE. Her work appears in various journals including *Social Science Computer Review*, *Social Science Quarterly*, and *Presidential Studies Quarterly*.

Deron T. Schreck is a professor of political science at Moraine Valley Community College in Palos Hills, Illinois. He teaches classes in American Government, state and local governments, and political philosophy. He earned his PhD in political science from the University of Illinois at Chicago.

Hillary C. Shulman is currently an assistant professor at Ohio State University in the School of Communication. Her current line of research investigates the role of informal political communication in the political engagement process. She has also published on topics that include the role of media in political conflict, deception, socialization, and ostracism.

Allison K. Wisecup is an assistant professor in the Department of Sociology at Radford University. She earned her PhD from Duke University with a focus on social psychology and medical sociology. Her research focuses on the question of consensus in the meanings that individuals ascribe to the social world. She also has research interests in gender inequality in sport and the scholarship on teaching and learning.

INDEX

NOTE charts/tables are indicated with "t" in page locator, 28t

abilities for political engagement, 6,
    104–12, 116–17
    defined, 90, 105
accessibility of political language,
    100–2, 103, 116, 174
adversarial communication, 108–9
Allen, I. Elaine, 78
Almond, Gabriel A., 91
American Political Science
    Association (APSA), 1, 51, 123
ANES. *See* National Elections
    Survey (ANES)
Aristotle, 14–15
assignments, in political science
    courses, 18–19, 60

Bachen, Christine, 149
Basehart, Harry, 92
blogs, 20, 21–2, 26, 28t, 30, 148
Bond, Robert M., 159
Bowling Alone (Putnam), 51
Brady, Henry, 112, 113

Caliendo, Stephen M., 6, 174
California State University system, civic
    education requirements in, 16
Campbell, David E., 126
Campus Compact, 98
Carnegie Political Engagement
    Project (PEP), 52, 57, 59, 61,
    62, 63, 83n2
Cennamo, Katherine, 127–8
Center for Information and
    Research on Civic Learning and
    Engagement (CIRCLE), 123
Chaffee, Steven, 105–6

Chod, Suzanne M., 6, 174
civic education
    college-level compared with
        primary/secondary levels,
        16–17
    in high schools, 13–14
    importance of, 14–17
civic engagement
    assessment of, 151, 152, 154,
        156–9, 156t, 157t, 158t
    communication interventions and,
        5–6
    compared to political
        engagement, 52, 61–2, 75–7
    decline of in Millennial
        generation, 1, 13
    defined, 51–2, 57–8, 62
    importance of civic education to,
        14–17
    necessary factors for, 89–90
    online activity and, 4, 20–2,
        149–50, 151, 174–6
    research on, 51–2, 177–8
    scale for, 62–3
    scientific approach to, 173–4
    See also government officials,
        contacting of; newspapers,
        contacting of; political
        groups, joining of; protests,
        participation in
civic norms, 91–7, 116
civic volunteerism model, 112
CLARIFY, 29, 31, 32t, 33t
Colby, Anne, 61–2, 63
college campuses, political activity
    at, 113–16, 117

college students. *See* Millennial
  generation
communication, 89–118, 177
  abilities and, 104–12
  adversarial, 108–9
  civic engagement and, 5–6, 175
  cooperative, 108–9, 110–11, 117
  opportunities and, 112–16
  political efficacy and, 97–104
  social norms and, 91–7
community college students, 138–9
confidence, 98, 99–100, 107, 116, 174
cooperative communication, 108–9,
  110–11, 117
Cooperative Institutional Research
  Program Freshman Survey, 13
Corbin, Tanya B., 4–5, 175–6
Craig, Stephen C., 98
current affairs knowledge and
  assignments, 150–1, 153

Dahl, Robert A., 15
Dalton, Russell J., 91–2, 94
de Vreese, Claes H., 125
Deliberative Learning Model
  (DLM), 106–7
Delli Carpini, Michael, 89–90,
  90–1, 96, 104, 112, 116
democracy
  citizen duty in, 91
  Millennial cynicism toward, 98,
    112–13
  political participation in, 15, 147
discussion boards, online, 150–9
Dream Act, 100–1
Driscoll, Adam, 74, 77
Dugan, Andrew, 23

economy, views on, as predictor of
  political activity, 24, 27, 28t,
  30, 41–2n3, 43n7
Ellison, Nicole B., 127
Ertmer, Peggy A., 127–8
external efficacy
  civic education's effect on, 16
  defined, 98, 133

Likert scale questions for, 134,
  135t, 137t
See also internal efficacy

Facebook, 7, 147–60
  vs online discussion boards,
    150–9
  social belonging and, 127
  use of by Millennials, 149–50
Flanagan, Constance, 14, 18

Gainous, Jason, 16, 18–19
Galston, William A., 125
gender, of respondents, 42n4, 60,
  67t, 69t, 70t, 72t, 132t
Gil de Zuniga, Homero, 21
GlobalWebIndex, 124
government officials, contacting of,
  42n6, 42n7, 175
  frequency of, 25
  interest in politics and, 24
  linkage to political science
    courses, 19, 27, 28t, 31, 32t,
    34
  online political activity and, 29
  political opinions and, 30
  students' expectations of, 62
GPA (grade point averages), 77
group membership, 113

health care, opinions on, 42–3n7,
  42n3
Heiberger, Greg, 129
high schools, civic education
  requirements in, 13–14,
    15, 16

interdisciplinarity, 5, 17, 19
interest in politics, 27, 28t
  Internet use and, 126
  political discussion research and,
    109–10
  as predictor of political activity,
    23–4, 30
  Twitter use research and, 133,
    134–6, 135t, 137t

internal efficacy
  civic education's effect on, 16
  defined, 98, 133
  Likert scale questions for, 133–4,
    135t, 137t
  political communication and,
    99–104
  scale for, 61
  See also external efficacy
introduction to American
    government courses, 73–4

Jackman, Jennifer, 56
Java, Akshay, 128
Jefferson, Thomas, 15
Jennings, M. Kent, 126
Johnson, Thomas J., 126
Jonassen, David, 127, 176
Junco, Reynol, 129
Junn, Jane, 16

Kahne, Joseph E., 16, 18–19
Kaye, Barbara E., 126
Kids Voting USA, 105–6
Kiousis, Spiro, 106, 107

Lampe, Cliff, 127
Levine, Peter, 14, 18
Levine, Timothy R., 114
Lewis-Beck, Michael, 24
Loken, Eric, 129

Madupalli, Ramana, 21
majors, choice of, as predictor of
    political activity, 24, 27, 28t, 30
Martens, Allison M., 16, 18–19
Mattei, Franco, 98
McCartney, Alison Rios Millett, 52,
    61, 62, 63
McDevitt, Michael, 105–6, 107
McDonaldization, 54
message personalization, 92, 96
Millennial generation
  centrality of Internet in lives of,
    20–1
  civic duty and, 91–2

civic vs political participation of,
    7–8
communication problem with,
    89–90, 117–18
decline in political activity of, 13
effect of economy on, 24
information acquisition by,
    100–1, 104, 125–6, 148
motivators for, 91–2, 95–7
political opportunities for,
    112–13
use of social media by, 148, 149
Min, Seong-Jae, 21, 56
Moffett, Kenneth W., 3–4, 21, 174
motivations for political
    engagement, 5–6, 90–104, 116
  defined, 90–1
  in deliberative learning
    model, 107
  political efficacy and, 97–104
  social norms and, 91–7
Muck, William J., 6, 174
Murray, Leah A., 7–8, 174, 175

Nagler, Peter, 92
National Association of Secretaries
    of State, 91–2
National Elections Survey (ANES),
    97, 102, 133
newspapers, contacting of, 175
  frequency of, 25, 33t
  interest in politics and, 24
  linkage to political science
    courses, 19–20, 28t, 31–2,
    33t, 34
  online political activity and,
    29–30
  as response variable, 27
  students' expectations of, 62
  See also online news reading
newspapers, knowledge of parental
    subscription to, 60, 67t, 69t,
    70t, 72t
Niemi, Richard G., 16, 98
*No Significant Differences
    Phenomenon, The* (Russell), 53

Obama, Barack
  2008 presidential campaign, 148
  opinions on policies of, 24, 27,
    28t, 30, 43n7
online education
  benefits of, 53–4
  civic engagement in, 4–5, 56–7
  components for, 127–8
  discussions in, 54, 56, 59, 150–9
  increase in, 49, 78
  research on, 53–5
online education, compared with
    face-to-face courses, 50, 175–6
  analysis of data on, 64–73
  data collection for, 58–60
  research on, 53–5
  student characteristics in, 77
  Twitter use in, 124
online news reading, 26, 28t, 29
  civic engagement and, 22
  political participation and, 125–6
  via social media, 128–9, 148, 153
online political activity
  frequency of, 26, 175
  offline civic engagement and, 4,
    20–2, 28t, 29, 174–5
  opportunities for political
    engagement, 6, 112–16, 117
  defined, 90

partisanship, as predictor of political
    activity, 23, 26–7, 28t, 30
peers, influence of on political
    activity, 22–3, 26, 28t, 30,
    93–6, 113
PEP (Political Engagement
    Project). See Carnegie Political
    Engagement Project (PEP)
Pew Research Center, 41n2, 102,
    125, 128–9, 148
political discussions
  in classroom settings, 18, 35, 103,
    105, 107
  as communication strategy, 96–7
  in the home, 60, 67t, 69t, 70t,
    72t, 105
  online, 130–1, 150–9

in research study, 108–12, 116–17
  See also communication
political diversity on campus, 115,
    116, 117
political efficacy, 97–104
  defined, 97
  external efficacy, 16, 98, 133,
    134, 135t, 137t
  importance of, 97
  internal efficacy, 16, 61, 98,
    99–102, 133–4, 135t, 137t
  political discussion research and,
    109–10
  Twitter use research and, 134–6
political engagement
  compared to civic engagement,
    52, 61–2, 75–7
  defined, 52, 63, 125
  Facebook use and, 149–50
  research on, 52
  scale for, 63–4
political groups, joining of
  frequency of, 25
  interest in politics and, 23–4, 30
  linkage to political science
    courses, 19–20, 28t, 29, 32, 34
political opinions
  formation of, 17–18
  political blogs and, 21–2
political science courses
  impact of, 17–20
  relationship with forms of civic
    engagement, 19–20, 28t, 31–6
politicized environments, 114–16,
    117
private schools vs public schools,
    115–16
protests, participation in
  frequency of, 25, 33t
  interest in politics and, 23–4, 30
  linkage to political science
    courses, 19–20, 27–9, 28t, 32,
    33t, 34
  online political activity and,
    29–30
  political opinions and, 30
  students' expectations of, 62

public opinion surveys, 101–2
Puig-I-Abril, Eulalia, 21
Putnam, Robert D., 49, 51,
    125, 175

Quality Matters (QM) training, 55

race, of respondents, 42n4, 60, 67t,
    69t, 70t, 72t, 132t
Rahn, W., 98
respondents, demographics of,
    42n4, 60, 132t–3
Rice, Laurie L., 3–4, 21, 174
Rojas, Hernando, 21
Ross, John D., 127–8
Rousseau, Jean-Jacques, 15
Russell, Thomas L., 53

same-sex marriage, opinions on,
    42–3n7, 42n3
Schlozman, Kay Lehman, 112, 113
Schreck, Deron, 6, 174
Seaman, Jeff, 78
selectivity of universities, 115
service learning, 1–2, 18, 35, 51, 56
Shulman, Hillary C., 5–6, 103, 108,
    109, 114, 175, 177
simulations, 18, 35
social belonging, Facebook use
    and, 127
social capital, 125, 130, 140, 175, 176
social constructivism, 127
social media
    influence of on political
        activity, 175
    Millennials' use of, 20–1,
        148, 174
    as news source, 126
    social capital and, 176
    See also Facebook; Twitter
social networks
    influence of on political activity,
        22–3, 26, 29
    instructors' use of, 148
    presidential campaign and, 148
    See also Facebook

social norms. See civic norms
Southern Illinois University, 24–5
Sporte, Susan E., 18
Steinfield, Charles, 127
Summers, Jessica J., 54
surveys, web-based, 24–5

technology, adoption of, 127–8,
    176
Texas, civic education requirements
    in, 15–16
Tocqueville, Alexis de, 147
transmission model of civic
    education, 106–7
Twitter, 6–7, 123–40
    anecdotal benefits of, 130–1
    effectiveness of, 136–8, 139–40
    instructor's use of, 139, 140
    Millennials' use of, 124
    for obtaining news, 128–9
    research study on use of, 131–9
    student engagement and, 129

Verba, Sydney, 91, 112, 113
volunteer work, 63, 77, 92
    knowledge of in the home, 60,
        66, 67t, 69t, 70t, 72t
voting
    civic duty as motivator for, 91–2
    college-level civic education and,
        16, 97, 113
    decline in by young people, 98,
        123
    knowledge of parental
        participation in, 60–1, 67t, 69t,
        70t, 72t
    social media and, 149, 159
    social norms and, 93

Washington, George, 15
Wellman, Barry, 21
Westheimer, Joel, 16
Wisecup, Allison K., 4–5, 175–6
Wittenbaum, Gwen M., 108, 109

Zeitner, Vicki, 126

GPSR Compliance
The European Union's (EU) General Product Safety Regulation (GPSR) is a set
of rules that requires consumer products to be safe and our obligations to
ensure this.

If you have any concerns about our products, you can contact us on

ProductSafety@springernature.com

In case Publisher is established outside the EU, the EU authorized
representative is:

Springer Nature Customer Service Center GmbH
Europaplatz 3
69115 Heidelberg, Germany